Take Your Library Workshops Online!

Take Your Library Workshops Online!

Anne Grant and Diana Finkle

ROWMAN & LITTLEFIELD
Lanham • Boulder • New York • London

Published by Rowman & Littlefield
A wholly owned subsidiary of The Rowman & Littlefield Publishing Group, Inc.
4501 Forbes Boulevard, Suite 200, Lanham, Maryland 20706
www.rowman.com

Unit A, Whitacre Mews, 26-34 Stannary Street, London SE11 4AB

Copyright © 2016 by Rowman & Littlefield Publishers, Inc.

All rights reserved. No part of this book may be reproduced in any form or by any electronic or mechanical means, including information storage and retrieval systems, without written permission from the publisher, except by a reviewer who may quote passages in a review.

British Library Cataloguing in Publication Information Available

Library of Congress Cataloging-in-Publication Data

Names: Grant, Anne, 1975– author. | Finkle, Diana, 1985– author.
Title: Take your library workshops online! / Anne Grant and Diana Finkle.
Description: Lanham : Rowman & Littlefield, [2016] | Includes bibliographical references and index.
Identifiers: LCCN 2016000786| ISBN 9781442263970 (hardcover : alk. paper) | ISBN 9781442263987 (pbk. : alk. paper)
Subjects: LCSH: Library orientation for college students—Web-based instruction. | Web-based instruction—Design. | Academic libraries—Relations with faculty and curriculum. | Libraries and colleges—United States—Case studies. | Clemson University.
Classification: LCC Z711.25.C65 G73 2016 | DDC 025.5/677—dc23
LC record available at https://lccn.loc.gov/2016000786

∞™ The paper used in this publication meets the minimum requirements of American National Standard for Information Sciences Permanence of Paper for Printed Library Materials, ANSI/NISO Z39.48-1992.

Printed in the United States of America

Contents

Acknowledgments — vii
Preface — ix

1. Saying Goodbye to the Face-to-Face Drop-In Workshop? — 1
2. Getting the Ball Rolling — 13
3. Gathering Intel: Finding Your Audience — 23
4. Creating the Synchronous Workshop — 35
5. Moving from Workshop to Tutorial — 53
6. Bringing Library Staff On Board — 73
7. Marketing Online Workshops — 83
8. Reaching Out to Faculty — 99
9. Assessing Online Instruction — 113
10. Summing It Up: Tips, Sample Plans, and Fitting into the Big Picture — 131

Appendix 1: Sample Focus Group Script and Question Sheet — 141
Appendix 2: Excerpt of Aggregated Data from Student Focus Groups — 145
Appendix 3: Sample Extension Agent Survey — 147
Bibliography — 151
About the Authors — 153

Acknowledgments

We would like to thank Micki Reid for the photographic contributions and Andy Wesolek for his insights into copyright in consultation on the content of this book. We also would like to express our appreciation of all our Clemson University Libraries colleagues who assisted during the years of effort about which we have written this book.

Preface

Are you nervous about declining attendance in your face-to-face workshops? Do you know that you need to make a change to your instruction program but are not sure how? We faced these same questions at our institution and started along a path of discovery that led us from square one to a program that provides both real-time and recorded online instruction. Through virtual classroom sessions, we opened up live instruction opportunities to students outside the library walls, whether they were at another campus site or in the comfort of their dorm rooms. Our online tutorials can be used to fill information and research needs anywhere at any time, whether within the learning management system during class time or via a YouTube search at 2 a.m.

Developing these online instruction solutions was not easy and involved a long process of gathering data, exploring technologies, investigating best practices, and discovering what did and did not work for our library, audience, and institution. We intend this book to be an honest discussion of much of this process as well as a guide of how to implement changes to instruction more effectively at your own institution. The book begins with a discussion of the motivating factors behind our shift online given an analysis of trends both at our institution and within the larger landscape of United States higher education libraries. Next, we walk you through ways of evaluating your unique campus need, establishing useful connections with other campus departments, and developing online instruction that is engaging, appropriate, and accessible. We then discuss how to assess, report on, and improve your content once it has been created. With down-to-earth discussions of our first-hand experiences, this book means you can learn from our experiences, examples, and errors.

We wrote *Take Your Library Workshops Online!* to serve as a guide for the academic librarian or library worker who is involved in library instruction, regardless of whether at a large university or a small technical college. It is intended as an introduction and how-to guide for anyone in that audience who is exploring the technical, pedagogical, and logistical considerations of establishing or improving online library instruction, and it includes workflows and detailed instructions as well as inclusive suggestions for marketing and technical solutions.

If you are interested in establishing or diversifying the online workshops available to your campus community, there is no need to begin at the very beginning. Learn from our experiences in creating an online workshop program, from examining the change in library instruction culture to determining the online content types most appropriate for your institution all the way through gathering feedback on these new efforts and applying that information to improvement and institutional reporting.

ONE
Saying Goodbye to the Face-to-Face Drop-In Workshop?

Providing a drop-in library workshop is not easy. First, you have to find a relevant topic that will attract participants and one that fits the talents of the library instructor who will lead the session. After you have a selected topic, you need to prepare an outline that will include sample searches, planned activities for an engaging lesson, outcomes, and assessments. Next, you need to find space in which to hold the workshop, considering whether your students will need individual computer access in a lab or a space conducive to group activities. Finally, you must put into action some type of marketing plan to raise awareness of the workshop among its targeted audience. This marketing plan will include choices about placement of marketing material that is crucial to the success of the awareness campaign. Should you put advertising online, in print, on social media, in direct-mail fliers, on bulletin boards, or all of the above? Whether in print or online, marketing pieces need to be attractive, eye catching, and direct. Much of the same is true about the session that you are planning to provide. Library instructors need to ensure that participants in their workshop are engaged, educated, and enlightened. Thus, before the students have even entered the classroom, you as the instructor or instruction coordinator have invested a great deal of effort into the session. You have put your time, energy, and creativity on the line before you are even guaranteed an audience. Therefore, when a drop-in workshop is prepared, advertised, and convened, it can be very disheartening for the library instructor when no one shows up, and it can be equally difficult when only one or two people attend a session. Although low attendance increases the one-on-one attention available for each student, it can also lead to a much different dynamic than expected by both the instructor and the student(s). These brave attendees often sit awkwardly during a session with interactions and activities designed for a much larger group. In either case, these kinds of results do not provide the return on investment that you need when creating an instructional opportunity. In the end, this scenario is beneficial neither to you nor the patrons since the time and energy you spent creating this poorly attended or cancelled session could have been used on another more desired area of service. Unfortunately, this scenario is uncomfortably common because the library instruction needs of modern academic patrons have changed in recent years. Steven Bell and John Shank, pioneers in the concept of the "blended librarian," attribute some of these changes to changes in the way textbook publishers include content from databases, major changes in scholarly publishing, and the "Googleization phenomena" that has led many library systems to become more user friendly.[1] More evidence of this shift online comes in the form of changing attendance in face-to-face library workshops, fewer requests for subject instruction, and in the changing expectations of academic library users. The good news as libraries take steps toward online instruction comes from studies like the one published in 2014 that was conducted with upper-level sociology undergraduates; evidence suggests that there was not much learning difference for students participating in online sessions and those held face-to-face.[2]

This book will describe the process of introducing online learning as a concept for traditional library instructors and will cover technological and pedagogical considerations for online classrooms as well as ideas for assessing the impact of this instruction. We as library instructors need to be proactive as we encounter new audiences and online programming that requires a different kind of information literacy intervention.

In this chapter, we will talk about ways to get the conversation started with a variety of library instructors; some will be more willing than others to venture into unknown or unfamiliar territory. Next, we will take you through the process of gathering some information about your particular audience, as each institution has a unique campus climate with its own opportunities and difficulties. In chapters 4 and 5, we will discuss specific methods for moving your workshops from face-to-face to online, both pedagogically and technologically. Then, once you have created these gems of online learning, you will need to know about how to market them to your audience, so we will cover some tips for raising awareness both internally and externally. Finally, we will include ideas for assessment with some specific tips from the field in our last two chapters. Overall, we hope to provide a foundation for beginning or revitalizing discussions at your library about migrating your excellent information literacy programming into an environment that makes it easy to find and useful for those who need it most.

MEETING YOUR STUDENT

Before we start talking about the changes in the academic library environment, we would like to introduce you to a typical university student. Please meet Jane Q. Student. Jane graduated with excellent grades from Anywhere High and has three Advanced Placement classes under her belt, which means she will not even have to take some of the introductory classes at Anywhere University, where she has just begun classes. She has endured the rigors of registration and summer orientation and is beginning her three-and-a-half-year (she plans to attend summer school) adventure. Jane spends a lot of time on her phone texting her mom about the class she just finished, FaceTiming with her best friend at a different university to catch up on what all their classmates are up to now, and Googling the latest news about her favorite actress, who has just announced her impending divorce. Jane feels confident in her ability to find information or at least to find quick tidbits of knowledge when she needs them that are good enough to get her the basic information. When she needs to know how to create a spreadsheet for her science lab, she decides to text her friend who had the class last year to find out the quickest way to create the best result. When she needs to find three journal articles for her next English paper, she heads straight to Google. When she is not sure if the articles she found will be good enough for her teacher, she asks the guy next to her in class how he found his sources. He mentions that the library has some ways to find information, so she opens the library webpage and tries the first search box she sees. When she encounters a problem, she uses the chat box on the page to ask for help because it is too much trouble—and a little embarrassing—to call or go and talk to someone. Jane is not someone who has a lot of time to waste. She has friends who she can ask for help and she already feels confident in her information-seeking ability. After all, she was smart enough to get into Anywhere University in the first place, was she not?[3] While Jane is a fictional sample user, she can offer a bit of insight into a world of college students who have little time or patience for attending an optional fifty-minute drop in library workshop that *might* teach them one new thing. Sure, they have heard that the campus librarians are friendly and helpful, but they would have to take an hour out of their busy schedules to go and sit in yet another classroom with the hope of getting the one or two pieces of information they need.

THE WRITING ON THE WALL

The fluctuation of attendance at library presentations is not a new, sudden, or isolated phenomenon. A comparison of Association of Research Libraries (ARL) statistics from 2006/2007 to 2012/2013 shows that while some ARL libraries have had dramatic increases or decreases in presentations and attendance, most are staying flat over this period.[4] Statistics gathered by the Association of Southeastern Research Libraries (ASERL) show quite a fluctuation with a general decrease in the number of presentations to groups.[5] These statistics may not directly reflect the library workshop per se, as the numbers most likely include any presentation made by the library such as orientations, tours, and other public appearances, but they do indicate changing patterns. With the increased ability to offer "just-in-time" instruction via online tutorials or chat interfaces, there is a new need for librarians to shift the way that we assess our instruction as well because numbers of attendance in workshops no longer directly reflects the impact of our teaching on our constituents. While we can breathe an initial sigh of relief that numbers have not declined noticeably during this period, these data are a bit troublesome within the larger environment of US higher education. The total number of undergraduate students in the United States continues to grow steadily and is expected to continue that trajectory into 2020 and beyond.[6] In light of the fact that colleges are serving an ever-increasing volume of full- and part-time students, this flat growth in library presentations and attendance seems a bit less reassuring.

Our own experience here at Clemson, combined with anecdotal evidence from other campus trainers and librarians within our state, indicates that patron interest in scheduled face-to-face instruction has declined precipitously. However, published admissions of this fact are hard to come by. Honestly, these shifting numbers are not something most librarians like to talk about since they can indicate, at least on the surface, that the need for library services is changing, and that can make many library instructors uncomfortable. The reality is increased access to the Internet for academic research at all grade levels, which has undoubtedly changed the perceived need of library patrons for instruction about access to resources, although this ease of access is a relatively new concept when compared to the long history of libraries. This familiarity with resource discovery (even when the resources may be of questionable quality) becomes evident once the average college student, who has grown up having access to the Internet, reaches a point where they need to begin their university-level research. This shift is not necessarily something to fear; it should be of no surprise that Internet access has profoundly affected the way students conduct research and the way that library instructors must adapt to teaching new research skills. Yet this audience of Internet savvy students is difficult to reach in the traditional fifty-minute face-to-face library instruction environment because, as evidenced by a research study in 2009, they have a very high level of confidence in their ability to find information online.[7] A student that feels no need to learn more about how to do research is unlikely to attend a just-in-case workshop designed to improve skills that they think they already have. On the other hand, when you teach a workshop that has been requested by a professor or incentivized with extra credit, students are often at best politely disinterested and at worst disruptive or resentful. If there were truly no need for this instruction, librarians could gladly appropriate resources to more worthy causes. Unfortunately, these students' confidence is largely unfounded as research has shown that they are just not as savvy as they might believe.[8] At the graduate level, it may not be that students are overconfident in their information seeking abilities; instead, they are more likely to be unaware of library services and resources.[9]

Another sign of the need to explore new library instruction methods is the steady decline in reference interactions for most higher education institutions in the United States. Since 2010, mean reference transactions have declined for three of the four Carnegie classifications tracked by the Association of College & Research Libraries (ACRL). Among our peer group of doctorate-granting institutions, transactions dropped 36 percent from 2010 to 2014.[10] When viewed against the backdrop of increasing student populations, this figure looks even worse. It is at this point that we are faced with two questions. A noticeably decreased amount of transactions surely translates into at least some decrease in reference workload, so what are we as library staff doing with that newly found free time? If the number of students is increasing yet the number of questions they ask us is in decline, what can we do to assist the segment of students that now self-fulfills their information needs? We freely admit these questions are based on some fundamental assumptions and an oversimplification of the interrelated factors. However, we fully believe they need to be asked not only as a self-assessment but also in preparation for the possibility that university administrators and local legislators, who have just enough time for such overview statistics, will ask them of us.

EXAMPLE FROM THE FRONT LINES

Clemson University is a public, land-grant university with strong undergraduate and graduate programs involving 19,459 full-time enrolled students as of 2014.[11] At Clemson Libraries, we have eleven research librarians who specialize in different majors and who teach both general and subject-specific information literacy sessions. As with many other academic libraries, we have been making changes to meet the new needs of our students. For example, after gathering data about the questions asked at the reference desk using the READ Scale, an instrument designed to track difficulty levels of questions asked, our librarians found a drop in both the total number of questions fielded at the desk and their overall rating of difficulty and labor intensiveness.[12] However, questions asked via email and in person while librarians were away from the desk ranked much higher on the READ Scale. Based on these changing statistics at our traditional reference desk, we elected to merge our public service points for reference and circulation. Clemson Libraries now provides a single library services desk with circulation staff members trained to answer basic reference questions and reference librarians who are able to carry out basic circulation tasks. By combining public service points and shifting their focus to these more detailed research questions, our librarians were able to focus more time on honing their online research guides and extending their outreach to faculty in their subject areas. Our reference staff has also increased our focus on our provision of chat research service, a program with usage that has more than doubled in less than a decade from 393 questions in 2006/2007 to 1,019 questions in 2014/2015. This statistic seems yet again to confirm that our constituents are opting more for the "just-in-time" online help. It is not just in an instructional environment that students seem to lean more toward last-minute self-service. Here at Clemson, we also offer online study room booking via our LibCal system in which students can and do regularly book rooms as needed online with only two hours' lead time.[13] Since the streamlining of online courses at Clemson under the Provost-supported Clemson Online initiative, the number of online courses at Clemson has also increased. More specifically, the number of online courses, as designated in our course registration system, rose more than 40 percent in two years, from 225 in the fall semester of 2013 to 319 in fall of 2015. Thus, with an increase in online programs and changing student search patterns, it is crucial to strive to meet the needs of students as they arise and in the online environment where they spend most of their time.

Other reasons for the decline in face-to-face library workshop attendance may also be due to lack of awareness about library services. In a world where students are inundated with a constant flow of information, it can be difficult to get the library message out to the academic community. With so many emails coming in, even the most targeted and well-crafted messages risk immediate deletion. This is especially true when members of an academic community already feel as though they are adept at information seeking and may be hesitant to ask for assistance in using new technologies or databases. Faculty also tend to take ownership of teaching critical thinking and research skills, including source evaluation, as they seek to guide their students in their disciplines and therefore do not call on librarians to teach these skills. In addition, both faculty and graduate students can be so overwhelmed with other academic obligations that they do not have time to investigate support opportunities ahead of time. Instead, they are often content just to get by with the information they are able to access at the last minute and via tools with which they are familiar. The Principle of Least Effort is as relevant today as it was in 1894 and students and faculty who are already overwhelmed with conflicting opportunities will often take the path that is easiest instead of the path that leads to the best information.[14] This desire for assistance in the moment, this just-in-time need, has significantly contributed to a decline in face-to-face workshops.

Requests from faculty for subject-specific instruction have also been changing during the past decade. For example, Clemson University Libraries taught 126 subject instruction sessions during the fall semester of 2006 and during fall of 2014, there were 87. Reasons for this decline could include anything from database interface improvements, advances in web search algorithms, and the confidence that comes from functioning daily in a digital age because all of these empower faculty to feel as if they can provide students with everything they need to know about searching for information. This trend is also not unique to Clemson. A 2011 study from York University in Canada found that of the faculty they surveyed about the integration of information literacy in their courses, 50 percent chose to teach these skills without a librarian while the other half did elect to collaborate with the library.[15] Since faculty members in particular are confident in their own abilities, they might see no benefit to having a librarian address their students. In turn, they may request fewer sessions from librarians who might come into their classroom and take up an entire classroom session, a session that might be crucial to their course timeline. Traditionally, library sessions for subject classes are fifty minutes to an hour and fifteen minutes. Anecdotally, librarians say that they prefer these longer classes so that they can provide more information. In these "typical" face-to-face sessions, librarians tend to teach students how to find and search effectively in library databases and about citation tools, along with tips for evaluating their sources and ways to avoid plagiarism. A hands-on activity where students are required to use the skills they acquired will probably be included and at the end of the session, they will have gained new skills that will help them complete their assignment. Some librarians have even worked with the flipped classroom concept so that they can spend more classroom time engaged in active searching, but this can mean twice the work for librarians, who must create both an online and a face-to-face learning experience.

Why else might subject-specific instruction sessions drop almost 50 percent from 2006 to 2015 at Clemson in particular? By all evidence, it was not due to a lack of quality in these sessions or their instructors. All feedback gathered from sessions indicated that faculty members were pleased with the information that their students received and that librarians continued to provide excellent instruction. Could it be that the online library guides created for classes and subjects (through LibGuides) provide all the information about resources and services that students might need for their projects? Students and faculty are more mobile than ever and use of handheld devices is at an all-time high, so is that where they are accessing information?

Providing library support for subject instruction can sometimes be challenging to segment and move to an online environment because it can be highly individualized. In addition, library instruction often depends on the demonstration of databases that frequently and unexpectedly undergo changes in interface design. Students conducting in-depth, subject-related research will have very specific needs that broad-based tutorials will not meet. When considering this, perhaps at this level of research it may be more appropriate to create online pieces that make students more aware of library services rather than the in-depth lessons on how to do tasks that are more specific. That way, students would be more aware of how to get help with specific questions when they need it rather than trying to create online instruction that attempts to anticipate student needs. As one study suggests, library liaisons might consider "increasing focus on what users do (research, teaching, and learning) rather than on what librarians do (collections, reference, library instruction)."[16] This concept feeds into the idea of blended librarianship that

Figure 1.1. Tweet of an empty classroom

was previously mentioned and will be discussed in more detail in chapter 6.

Even with workshops that are required, attendance can be an issue, and although they may be attending the workshops, it does not necessarily mean that the students are walking away with new skills and abilities. Beginning with the fall semester of 2008, the Clemson Libraries had an opportunity to participate in a required, zero-credit orientation course for all incoming students. As a part of this course, the library provided a fifty-minute face-to-face workshop designed to introduce students to the resources and services available from the libraries on campus. Clemson librarians taught approximately two hundred sessions each fall semester, which reasonably calculates to an investment of at least two hundred hours. These sessions, taught using an outline provided by the instruction coordinator, were evaluated in a few different ways, but it was difficult to ascertain the value to students who were learning about the library within their first couple of weeks on campus during a session that was not tied to a specific course or assignment. With no concrete relevance to students' needs at the time and no motivating factor beyond the desire to avoid failing a zero-credit course, the library portion was a tough sell. In the summer of 2011, the instruction coordinator began conversations as to whether these sessions could be replaced with online tutorials since it seemed from the assessment gathered that students were walking away with a basic introduction to the library at best. This would enable the library to introduce basic library knowledge in a fraction of the time it took to lead those two hundred hours of face-to-face instruction. Librarians would be free to plan higher-level workshops for upper-level students and faculty. However, the decision to shift to online instruction was difficult to make because it meant that our statistics would reflect two hundred fewer workshops than we did the previous year, even though we were still essentially reaching the same number of students. This is especially relevant since instruction statistics often play a large role in the status of a library. Falling instruction statistics can mean a change in academic category.

You might be tempted to view this diminishing number as an indication of the decreased need for library instruction, funding, personnel, or all three. It is possible to employ alternative metrics to measure "attendance" in online library instruction and you should consider these possibilities as more online instructional pieces are developed. Regardless of whether library instruction at the subject level remains in a face-to-face or an online environment, it is crucial for librarians to understand the changes in the needs of faculty and students.

10   Chapter 1

SHIFTING NEEDS AND EXPECTATIONS

The needs of students and faculty are changing with the advent of faster, newer, more user-friendly information technology tools. Expectations of speed and individualization are on the rise as patrons have become accustomed to finding what they need easily in a format that will not dominate a great deal of precious time and energy. A study from 2011 noted that "students prized dependable, easily available information over less open campus-based resources," reinforcing the concept that in a modern university environment, convenience is inextricably linked to the online world.[17] Many times, you may find that students would rather chat anonymously or watch a very short YouTube video rather than speak with a person face-to-face. Other studies have shown that college students are frustrated with their access to scholarly resources and that students will often settle for mediocre sources rather than try to figure out how to use databases.[18] Yet, often students do not seek workshops for needs that they do not realize that they even have. The idea of spending fifty minutes in a class where a participant may walk away with one or two relevant pieces of information just does not seem to be where stu-

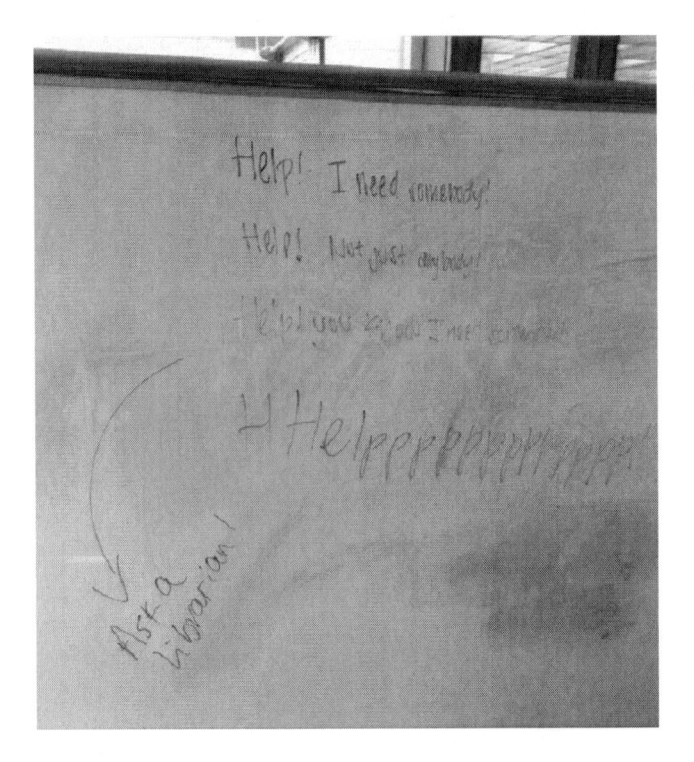

Figure 1.2.   Help! I need somebody! Whiteboard. *Photo by Micki Reid*

dents and faculty want to spend their time. Yet in surveys about library use, those questioned often request these very workshops and frequently indicate that they are unaware of the services and resources provided by the libraries.[19] The library and technology departments on campus often overlap when it comes to training and the two tend to go hand in hand when it comes to the needs of students and faculty. However, face-to-face technology classes face many of the same problems as the libraries in that the just-in-time instruction provided in the form of short videos (which you often find online being provided nonprofessionally by twelve-year-olds on YouTube) are gaining popularity by academic audiences over the just-in-case sessions that are usually longer and less individualized. Students also often believe they are more information literate than they actually are, a fact that can contribute to decreased attendance because a student who does not see a need to improve their skills will be less likely to seek to develop these skills.[20]

The library instruction needs of academic patrons have changed in the last ten years as evidenced by lower attendance at organized library workshops, fewer requests for face-to-face subject instruction, and indicators of the changing expectations of speed and ease of access from both students and faculty. In order to reach participants once again and provide these relevant and valuable research skills, libraries must find ways to adapt their teaching and delivery to meet these changes. You cannot do this by merely moving existing face-to-face sessions to an online environment. Librarians can rest assured that no one wants to sit through a fifty-minute instruction session online about the merits of doing effective research. First, research shows that academic patrons already feel as though they are adept at this skill even though they are not. Second, modern attention spans will not stand for such a lengthy session. Librarians will have to resist the urge to teach everything they can about a topic and instead condense small pieces of instruction into easily disseminated and digested segments of online learning that can be accessed at a point of need rather than being offered before the patron even knows that a need exists for that information. Online library instruction, whether provided in live sessions or in tutorials, provides access to research help in a just-in-time environment.

NOTES

1. Steven Bell and John Shank, "The Blended Librarian," *College & Research Library News* 65, no. 7 (2004): 373.

2. Amanda Hess, "Online and Face-to-Face Library Instruction," *Behavioral & Social Sciences Librarian* 33, no. 3 (2014): 141.

3. "New Insights on Characteristics of U.S. College Students," accessed November 10, 2015, http://monitor.icef.com/2012/12/new-insights-on-characteristics-of-us-college-students/.

4. Martha Kyrillidou and Les Bland, *ARL Statistics 2006–2007*, 141. Martha Kyrillidou, Shaneka Morris, and Gary Roebuck, *ARL Statistics 2012–2013*, 141.

5. ASERL Library Trend Report, accessed November 20, 2015.

6. Total Fall Enrollment in Degree-Granting Postsecondary Institutions, by Attendance Status, Sex of Student, and Control of Institution: Selected Years, 1947 through 2024, Digest of Education Statistics: 2013, National Center for Education Statistics, accessed November 24, 2015, http://nces.ed.gov/programs/digest/d14/tables/dt14_303.10.asp.

7. Melissa Gross and Don Latham, "Undergraduate Perceptions of Information Literacy," *College & Research Libraries* 70, no. 4 (2009): 336.

8. Melissa Gross and Don Latham, "What's Skill Got to Do with It? Information Literacy Skills and Self-Views of Ability among First-Year College Students," *Journal of the American Society for Information Science and Technology* 63, no. 3 (2012): 582.

9. Amy Catalano, "Patterns of Graduate Students' Information Seeking Behavior," *Journal of Documentation* 69, no. 2 (2013): 269.

10. Kyrillidou and Bland, *ARL Statistics 2006–2007*, 141. Kyrillidou, Morris, and Roebuck, *ARL Statistics 2012–2013*, 141.

11. "Mini Fact Book 2014," Clemson University, accessed November 10, 2015, http://www.clemson.edu/oirweb1/FB/factbook/minifactbook.cgi.

12. "The READ Scale: Reference Effort Assessment Data," accessed November 9, 2015, http://readscale.org/.

13. LibCal, *Springshare*, http://springshare.com/libcal/.

14. Guillaume Ferrero, "L'inertie mentale et la loi du moindre effort," *Revue philosophique de la France et de L'étranger* 37 (1894): 169–82.

15. Sophie Bury, "Faculty Attitudes, Perceptions and Experiences of Information Literacy: A Study across Multiple Disciplines at York University, Canada," *Journal of Information Literacy* 5, no. 1 (2011): 59.

16. Janice Jaguszewski and Karen Williams, "New Roles for New Times," Report prepared for the Association of Research Libraries. http://www.arl.org/storage/documents/publications/nrnt-liaison-roles-revised.pdf (2013): 4.

17. J. Patrick Biddix, Chung Joo Chung, and Han Woo Park, "Convenience or Credibility?," *The Internet and Higher Education* 14, no. 3 (2011): 180.

18. Denise R. Denison and Diane Montgomery, "Annoyance or Delight?: College Students' Perspectives on Looking for Information," *The Journal of Academic Librarianship* 38, no. 6 (2012): 3 88.

19. "Measuring Information Services Outcomes (MISO)," accessed June 21, 2015, http://www.misosurvey.org/.

20. Melissa Gross and Don Latham, "Experiences with and Perceptions of Information: A Phenomenographic Study of First-Year College Students," *The Library Quarterly: Information, Community, Policy* 81, no. 2 (2011): 184.

TWO
Getting the Ball Rolling

For centuries, the library has been *the* place to go for students to find information, but as students rely more heavily on Internet searches for their research, this has been changing.[1] Yet, often library instruction programs focus on teaching to students and faculty who are actively seeking face-to-face instruction on using library resources. This instruction has been traditionally isolated in that it is created within the library by librarians who do their best to seek feedback from their constituents. Perhaps because of this isolation, this instruction has also tended to speak to what the library has to offer rather than concentrating on the task that the student or faculty member is trying to accomplish. For example, you may have seen or taught a library workshop that claims to "teach students how to use library databases to find better research"; and while this session may very well accomplish this goal, the actual need that students might have is to "find sources at the last minute that will make a research paper better."

In the case of many undergraduates, the actual need may even be closer to helping students filter the information they have already found to determine the best sources.[2] At any rate, one of the keys to the true need of students is the "last-minute" stipulation, because students, and even some faculty members and librarians (gasp), have been known to wait until the last minute to complete a project! This tendency is enabled by the fact that many of the resources that they may need are accessible 24/7 via the web or even within libraries that may be open all night during the week. With access to materials both on and off campus, instructional options should be available as well on the same basis and within the online environment where the research is happening. These online workshops can serve as an option for those who do not have physical access to the library, but we are not contending that they should replace all face-to-face sessions because those remain crucial to students and faculty alike. So, keeping this in mind, unless you want to begin making yourself available 24/7 (as some have done via chat consortiums), online instruction pieces are helpful to work toward this goal. You can begin to plan a selection of online workshops by finding partners and support, determining what existing library instruction content is suited for the online environment, and starting conversations with library instructors.

THE PERFECT PARTNER(S)

Librarians are always working diligently to seek out partners in their endeavor to create an academic support team for students. One of the most difficult challenges you might face when beginning to seek out new opportunities is the undeniable truth that resources are finite. Unfortunately, each opportunity to create a new workshop series or event does not come bundled with a newly funded position or employee that wants to add even more to their workload (for the same amount of money). You may have found that your more enthusiastic library staff members are the ones willing to take on new challenges with instruction, but these are the same ones that already feel overwhelmed by existing commitments that have accumulated over the years. Then there is the daunting reality that sometimes, despite the best planning and partnerships, these events and workshops can fail to attract an audience. The key is to keep trying.

Teaching with Technology

A natural partner for libraries can be the campus technology trainers. These are the folks who offer workshops, either face-to-face or online, on hardware and software products. Many times, you will find that these technology instructors already have an existing framework for offering instruction via a registration system and they will also be familiar with the online classroom environment. A great way to leverage their skills and add library content is to create cooperative sessions. Some examples of "combination platter" workshops with the potential to move online might be the following:

- Create a research poster—the technology department provides instruction on the technical aspects of designing and printing the poster while the librarians provide instruction on finding the best research to display.
- Managing your data—the technology department provides instruction on the advanced use of Excel, SPSS, or other programs used on campus while the librarian describes the best way to access and store large data sets

Getting the Ball Rolling 15

Waiting for the stars to align to complete your final project?

Stop by our table staffed with writing fellows and research librarians to get help with finding research, making citations, and brushing up your writing style.

Best of all, you'll leave that much closer to a complete paper!

GET IT, WRITE IT, CITE IT!

Wednesday, December 2nd
8 -10pm
Cooper Library 6th Floor

CLEMSON UNIVERSITY
Writing Center

CLEMSON
LIBRARIES

Figure 2.1. Sample Quarter-Page Promotional Flyer

- Maximize course reserves—instruction on best practices for providing students access to course reserves through the institution's learning management system can be provided by the technology trainers, while reserve policies and procedures and copyright compliance information can be shared by library instructors
- Data visualization—technology instruction on the use of graphic design software or infographic services can be enhanced with library instruction on ensuring that the data being visualized is accurate and scholarly.
- Social media citizenship—technology professionals can discuss safety and security issues with online social networks while librar-

ians emphasize critical thinking skills needed to evaluate posts before sharing.

Writing Center

The writing center is a potential partner along with a suggestion of a writing lock-in where students commit to spending a couple of hours writing and researching their papers or project with writing center and library staff on hand to help with any questions. It can be difficult for you to even contemplate partnering with the writing center on campus to provide a research lock-in from 8 p.m.–10 p.m. (a prime time for students to be in the library during midterms or exam week) since it involves convincing a librarian who normally works days to stay until 10 p.m. This kind of opportunity has online potential, as librarians could be available via chat or Skype during the session, which would both allow for the anonymous, online help that students sometimes seek as well as the potential flexibility of allowing your staffers to work from anywhere. You will also need to consider the marketing, scheduling, registration management, and planning that you would have to put into the preparation of this kind of event as you plan your collaboration and distribution of tasks. Other ideas for partnering with your writing center include the following:

- Create a satellite station for writing center tutors in the library during busy times of the semester and emphasize online features for help from librarians via chat or online guides.
- Staff a "Get It, Write It, Cite It" table to provide last-minute help to students working on essays and other assignments and advertise online research help pieces available from the library.
- Design a LibGuide or other online-access tool with embedded links to instructional opportunities for writing center tutors to use as they work with students.
- Offer a "Writing Your Paper Right" workshop where a writing center representative provides tips for paper structure and formatting while librarians offer help on finding the best sources, either online or in person.

Office of Sponsored Programs (Grant Writing Support on Campus)

Another possible partner might be representatives from your institution's grant writing or research office. Again, this office may already be set up to register and market events to important constituent groups like faculty members and graduate students. This kind of partnership can allow librarians to become a more integral part of the grant writing process for both faculty and graduate students, a process that often involves inserting a key component of the grant that mentions library support for projects. Librarians also provide key support in data management plans and can work with faculty members to determine best practices for handling and storing their data, a component often required of many federally funded grants. In fact, many libraries are working to develop positions specifically geared toward addressing the data management needs of researchers and providing plan consultation and review services. This process is also one that might be carried out off campus and by providing online access for just-in-time help, which may appeal to faculty members in the throes of a project and unable to get to a scheduled session on campus. Examples for possible partnerships in this area might include

- Find your PubMed Central Reference Number (PMCID)—anyone publishing research funded by the National Institute of Health must include its PMCID and the library could create an online component to complement existing training that can be referred to later to effectively meet just-in-time needs.
- Research support for principle investigators (PI)—faculty and graduate students are often largely unaware that librarians can be extremely helpful in providing research support requirements for certain grants.
- Finding grant money—not only can librarians provide guides to print and electronic resources for possible grant funding, they can also become proficient in searching grant funding databases like InfoEd SMARTS.
- Creating a data management plan (DMP)—librarians are the information experts on campus and online sessions that specifically define DMPs as well as processes involved could be quite useful.

Career Center

The campus career resource office is also a key potential partner for libraries. Not only can the library assist in collecting resources for students, faculty, and staff to access in the collection, but they can also provide online guides to supplement the information provided in the campus career center. Teaming up for workshops with a specific purpose in mind can also be useful:

- Resume writing for professionals—career center reviewers can offer hints and tips while librarians provide links and resources from reliable sources.
- Cover letters that get you noticed—combine tips from career center representatives with the library's top resources on professional writing.

Academic Success Center

Centers providing academic support for students usually have a need for instruction on plagiarism and copyright and librarians serve a very important role on campus as the information experts. These kinds of workshops also hold a great deal of potential for the online environment as they offer many ways to incorporate interactivity by asking students to provide feedback on writing samples. Also, many well-done online modules already exist and are openly available for reuse, so librarians may even consider using these online pieces to flip sessions and ask students to view the basic rules before coming to a live session to make some real time determinations about proper use of citations.

Special Events

The library can also serve as a hub for events by pulling together research sessions from a variety of sources into one event. One way that we have done this here at Clemson is by hosting a "Grad Student Boot Camp," which began as a day-long, conference-style event with a variety of sessions and lunch included. We have also offered a shorter version where fifteen minute 'lightning rounds' from different campus resources provided students with information on resources and then they had a focused three hours to work on their projects with people there to help if needed. Sessions were offered by the writing center, the graduate school, campus technology trainers, librarians, and the career center. Students were provided with an opportunity to meet with their subject librarians and were given library t-shirts after evaluations were completed. This event could be streamed, although we have not moved in that direction yet, as many graduate programs are beginning to host online courses and programs or some have students who work in remote labs. These sessions can also be advertised to students who are planning to move on to graduate school and could incorporate sessions on writing entrance letters and completing graduate school applications.

Other Student Groups

You might also consider seeking out special student groups on campus. The honors college usually houses students who may be interested in targeted instructional opportunities. This could come in the form of special chat or Twitter hours where you can field questions or poll students for topics that they would like to see made into brief tutorials. Another group you might consider is athletes; by doing so, you could work with the programs that academically support athletes to design specialized sessions for different sports teams that speak to their games and help them relate that back to information seeking. Similarly, you might also reach out to the Greek organizations on campus to see if the library could work with them on compiling workshops that will fulfill any academic requirements as well as any needs students might have for their assignments. Student government groups are also excellent collaborators as these highly motivated students can serve as advisors to their peers as they direct them to library resources. Often, all it takes is asking to speak at one of their meetings each semester to help them understand more about the services and resources that the library provides.

Much like the libraries, many other support entities on campus have tended to be quite insular when it comes to providing training. Providing connection points and "one-stop-shopping" opportunities for campus constituents can be invaluable to instructors and students alike. When you shift instruction topics to speak to the needs of students and faculty members rather than what the library and librarians can teach, you can change the way that both partners and the campus see the role of the library. On many campuses, the library is still seen as a book box: there to store information but not necessarily to share or manage that information. Working with partners can assist in dispelling this notion, allowing libraries to lead the way with innovative teaching techniques and unique learning opportunities.

DECIDING WHICH CONTENT TO MOVE ONLINE

One of the key factors when moving content online is to consider the time factor. Just-in-time help online should be brief and to the point. Luckily, much of the content already exists in library instruction programs; it just needs to be broken into smaller pieces. For example, if you are a science librarian who teaches a session on finding and evaluating scientific research, a somewhat typical fifty-minute face-to-face session, you may consider creating an online series of tutorials instead of a one-time session. Topics could include

- Tips for using SciFinder
- Top five things to consider when evaluating a scientific article
- Three best databases for finding the most scholarly research in the sciences
- Tips for using Web of Science
- Organizing scientific resources using EndNote (or RefWorks or Mendeley)

It also may be possible for you to find tutorials that have already been created by someone else that you could link to from their subject or course guides. It is a good idea to go out and watch what others have done with similar tutorials anyway. A simple YouTube or Google video search will lead to numerous examples and in doing this it is possible to critique and decide which online teaching methods work best for individual student and/or faculty audiences.

It is also important to realize that teaching online is quite different from teaching face-to-face. One of the biggest differences is if you chose to record your sessions, once created and posted, online instruction can be seen from anywhere in the world and can be watched over and over again. This can be greatly beneficial, but it also needs to be treated carefully as the sessions can become outdated quickly and can lead patrons in the wrong direction.

STARTING AN AWKWARD CONVERSATION

Moving traditional library instruction online is not easy. Often those teaching face-to-face sessions have been doing so for a very long time and many have never had any experience in the online teaching environment or with creating or planning web-based tutorials. Librarians in this position can become quite uncomfortable and in the process can be resistant to participating in online initiatives. Thus, an important step for an instruction coordinator to take is to recognize and validate these concerns. Begin the process with open communication and a safe environment for instructors to voice opinions and thoughts and respect the different strengths that each library instructor brings to the table. If one or two library instructors who are keenly interested in teaching online can be identified, you can start with a small group and keep their progress (and struggles) out in the open for all to see. Then you can begin a larger conversation in open meetings guided with questions that are sent out beforehand. Some questions might include

- If you were going to create five short "library tips" tutorials, what would they address?
- Do you see yourself using the tutorials in your teaching? If so, how? If not, why not?
- How do you think the drop-in library workshops are going? What would you change? What would you leave the same?
- Would you teach a workshop online? Why or why not?
- What strategies do you use in the classroom (face-to-face or online) to teach about library resources?
- What kind of support do you need with regard to instruction (either face-to-face or online)?
- How should we create best practices and policies for our LibGuides so that we can ensure consistency and timely updates?

As these conversations and meetings take place, you need to be prepared for varying energy from those in attendance. Some may be emotional and agitated, while other will be excited and eager. It is also possible that you, as a leader of this kind of meeting, will be met with silence, a silence that can sometimes be broken by helping the group to focus on the true needs of students and faculty and how the library might best meet those needs. You can also use feedback from face-to-face sessions to help drive the conversations about possible transitions as your instructors may feel more secure when speaking of things of which they are more familiar. You can do this by bringing samples of feedback received from face-to-face sessions to stimulate conversation and this can lead to discussions about general best practices for teaching and ways to improve effectiveness in delivery of information both in subject sessions and in general library information sharing opportunities. Then, if nothing else, you have facilitated a discussion about improving teaching from the library instructors as a whole even in face-to-face sessions.

The transition to just-in-time, online instruction begins with a number of conversations and some of these conversations you may find to be quite difficult. The inclusion of academic and social partners from across campus, determining what existing content can be effectively and efficiently moved to the online environment, and then facilitating internal dialogue are all key components to changes of this nature. The role of the instruction coordinator is to maintain a safe and productive environment for these conversations and the role of those teaching is to keep the conversation moving and to keep open minds about what is best for the audiences who are utilizing library services. Honestly, online instruction will not always be the answer because you will still find that there is a need and a place for traditional, face-to-face library instruction. There is also a place for integrated and targeted subject instruction and one of the things that moving some of the basic library instruction pieces online can do is to free up time for librarians to focus on these more in-depth instructional opportunities. Library instructors may also have more of an opportunity to flip instruction by allowing students to review basic library skills outside of the classroom, leaving the face-to-face time for applied, hands-on activities.

NOTES

1. Kristen Purcell, et al., "How Teens Do Research in the Digital World," Pew Research Center, 2012, accessed November 20, 2015. http://www.pewinternet.org/2012/11/01/how-teens-do-research-in-the-digital-world/: 3.
2. Arthur Taylor, "A Study of the Information Search Behaviour of the Millennial Generation."

THREE
Gathering Intel

Finding Your Audience

It can be tempting for librarians to think that they instinctively know what is best for students and faculty. While librarians undoubtedly gain some natural insight into patron needs through regular face-to-face or virtual reference work, it is critical that instruction aligns with the needs of students and faculty since instruction programs can only be powerful if they address the audience's actual needs as well as possible. In other words, a student might *think* he is proficient at searching for scholarly information but in actuality only knows basic Google search skills. This kind of patron will not be interested in attending an "Advanced Google Searching Class" two months before his first project is due, partially because in his mind he is already proficient with Google. It may only be when he writes his paper (or perhaps even compiles his list of resources after having finished everything else) and finds his sources lacking that he goes in search of some help completing his bibliography. Unfortunately, he may reach this point at three o'clock in the morning when there is no librarian online or session taking place. He may turn to YouTube and type in something like "how to finish a bibliography." What if librarians were able to follow this kind of behavior and create instruction pieces that would appear in his YouTube results? It would certainly help us to create targeted learning objects that we know would be useful. Information about patron search patterns can be difficult to gather and will vary from institution to institution, but there are ways librarians can get a glimpse into their thoughts through the use of focus groups, individual consultations, and anonymous web-based feedback mechanisms.

Chapter 3
GATHERING OF THE MINDS

Focus groups can be tricky. To maximize your return on investment, you must do a significant amount of planning before you even begin that hopeful search for participants. The first consideration is what information you want to collect. Obviously, you want to learn about students' instruction needs; however, asking them that question outright is unlikely to produce much more than awkward silence. Instead, questions about how students currently seek help, especially at the last minute when it is most crucial, can provide valuable insight about where library information might be integrated. You may also want to find out about their existing technology access, preferred communication methods, and the times of day most commonly reserved for schoolwork. Since you also should collect basic demographic data and make the session conducive to thoughtful interaction, you may need to pare your question list or at least accept that you might not reach the end of it.

The second consideration is exactly how, where, and when you will collect your information. It requires significant multitasking skills to simultaneously lead and take notes on the interaction, so you may wish to use technology (e.g., iPhone, iPad, digital voice recorder) to record the session or recruit a colleague to be your scribe. The location you choose should be large enough to accommodate your group but small enough to foster open, give-and-take interaction. It should also be quiet enough, especially if you need a serviceable recording to work from later, yet not in an area where noise restrictions prevent comfortable conversation. As for choosing when to hold sessions, scheduling can affect both participation levels and data gathered. Different times of day and days of the week can attract very different participants. Furthermore, if students are questioned at the beginning of the semester about their research needs and habits, they will likely respond quite differently from when they are in the throes of completing their midterm research paper.

The next task is simply gathering a group of participants who are willing to spare some of their time and engaged enough to take the session seriously and volunteer honest information about their thoughts, ideas, and study habits. Ideally, this group of willing participants is also diverse enough to provide a broad and representative sample of your users. For example, you cannot expect to learn the needs of all undergraduates at your coeducational institution by talking with a group that is only comprised of females in their first year as computer science majors. Although prescreening participants with an in-person or online survey can allow you to approximate a random and representative sample, it may prove more demanding than the average participant (and facilitator) is willing to bear.

At the heart of all focus group preparation is the assumption that you will be able to attract an adequate number of participants. While the expectations for "adequate" depend largely on your resources and campus culture, each session should have at least a few participants with "a few" being defined as more than three but less than twelve. You can also opt for a more intense session by conducting a dyad, a qualitative research method often used in market research for collecting data with an interviewer and two respondents, or a triad in which a moderator would interview three respondents. These environments can produce some fast-paced and intense feedback and you may want to consider using a moderator from outside the library, perhaps even a student or faculty peer, depending on the participant demographic, since external interviewers might be less intimidating and encourage honest responses. For example, if a participant begins to discuss a problem they are having with a library service, the library staff member's instinct might be to suggest solutions instead of asking for more information about the problem. The use of peers as moderators in focus groups might also produce follow-up questions that might not be considered by those internal to the library.

Regardless of your focus group size, the abstract promise of improved library instruction is unlikely to entice many students to give up thirty or more minutes of their day, so how will you attract participants? Anyone who has been lured to a meeting by the promise of free cake can attest to the fact that rewards, even small ones, matter. For those with generous budgets, finding an enticing participant reward should be no trouble. Unfortunately, the answer to this may depend more on your budget than on what you think the average student would really enjoy. When faced with limited resources, the librarian must be a bit more thoughtful and creative. A morning session could advertise free coffee and pastries while a noon meeting could include a slice or two of pizza. For small groups, each participant might receive a low-denomination gift card for a nearby coffee shop. For very large participant pools, conducting a random drawing for one larger prize might be the most cost-effective solution. The librarian with no funding could offer the chance to win a guaranteed or preferential version of an existing resource. If space is at a premium during exam week, a table or study room reservation could be more valuable than any token compensation.

Beyond the intrinsic difficulties of planning and execution is the consideration of institutional compliance. Prior to conducting any focus groups, you may need to seek approval for your plans from the institutional research board (IRB), which regulates the safety of students involved in research on campus. Participants may need to provide informed consent by signing a waiver or acknowledgement. The study method or planned incentives may also need approval from a unit or department supervisor. Of course, a simple series of question-and-answer sessions may not be subject to any procedural or reporting requirements. If there is no need for IRB approval, it is still a good idea to disclose the study purpose, anonymity assurances, data use, and other important aspects to participants to create an environment of openness and encourage their quid pro quo honesty.

Figure 3.1 represents a basic workflow for actually conducting a focus group session. Much of it is self-explanatory and the exact order is more a suggestion than a prescription. You should definitely introduce yourself as well as anyone else you have invited to sit in or help with the session. If you know you are hosting a small group, you may want to do this as participants come in; otherwise, it would be easier to do it all at once after they are settled. This is your first opportunity to build a feeling of trust with your participants, which will be crucial as you get into the question and answer phases. Next, you will at the very least want to take count of how many participants you have. This is a good time to have them sign in if you had them preregister (with or without prescreening). If you plan to record the question and answer portion anyway, you may want to start the session recording just before you explain the purpose and expectations of the focus group session. If you are required to have participants give informed consent, this would be the time to make sure those forms are signed. When administering all of your questions, it is important to seem attentive but completely free of judgment. If you need to ask clarifying questions, use the same considerations for precision and understandability that you used when writing your original question list. You may find you need to interrupt a participant due to time constraints or other considerations. It might be awkward, but you will need to be kind but firm; you may want to invite the person to finish talking about that issue after the session or via email. If multiple participants get off track discussing their opinions or experiences, you can express your appreciation for their engagement but let them know you must move on since there

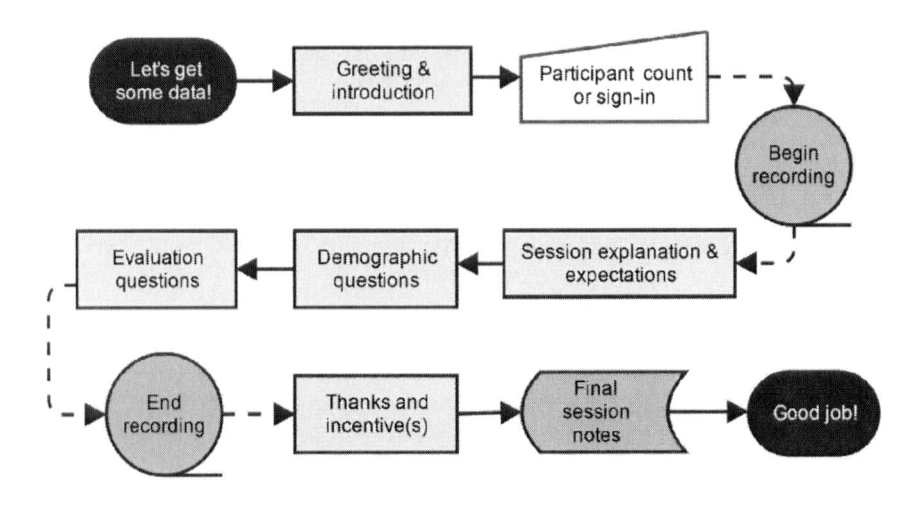

Figure 3.1. Sample Workflow for Conducting a Focus Group

are certain questions you need to get through for the session. Once you conclude the session and your participants have left, be sure to take down any final impressions. This is especially important if you do not record the session and are leading multiple groups, since it can be easy to forget details or confuse sessions.

PUTTING PLANS INTO ACTION

At Clemson during the spring semester of 2014, we decided to conduct student focus groups during exam week. Why did we pick then? One reason is that we hoped to gain participants by capitalizing on students' desire for a productive distraction from studying. Another reason is we could take the summer to apply the feedback gained to existing and new online offerings. In all honesty, however, the main reason for this timing was the fact that we had fifteen ten-dollar gift cards left over from another project and needed to find a way to distribute them before our institutional deadline. The specifics of this opportunity meant that several aspects about the configuration of these focus groups were already determined. Specifically, there would be no time or incentive available for students to undergo prescreening. Since recruitment for the sessions would be through existing communication media, participants would be students that already visit the library, view our social media or blog, or associate closely with someone who does. Limited personnel availability meant that one library staff member would be responsible for both leading and recording the group discussion. This, coupled with the predetermined value of the incentives, lead us to aim for sessions that lasted no more than thirty minutes. To accommodate students that may have a class during one of our scheduled sessions, we offered them multiple times and days. We chose three sessions because it seemed a reasonable compromise between too little choice and too much investment of staff time. Three sessions also meant we had incentives available for sessions of up to five participants each; five seemed ideal because it would be a small enough group to allow personal expression but not so small as to feel awkward. It would also result in a manageable number of people in the modest space we had available for hosting the groups. Since we wanted to make participation as easy as possible by not requiring preregistration, we had no way to know how many participants to expect. If an excessive number arrived, having multiple sessions would allow us to ask for volunteers that could return to a later session. The three sessions offered were on a Wednesday at 1 p.m. and the following day at both 10 a.m. and 2 p.m.

In planning the session content, we began by brainstorming what we would like to learn from the students. We then formed this list into a set of clear, succinct questions that we believed could be covered during thirty minutes. Because two people were available to lead groups, we drafted an introduction script to ensure consistency and that all the necessary information was covered. We also researched and prepared focus group consent forms to be signed by each participant just before the questioning began. Before posting any event information publicly, we distributed the information to our circulation and reference desk personnel and emailed members of our unit so they would be prepared in advance for any questions that might arise. We advertised these sessions via a whiteboard in the lobby facing the main entrance, two blog posts, and social media posts of the whiteboard photo on Facebook, Twitter, and Instagram.

We also posted 8.5" x 11" color flyers at the circulation and reference desks, in elevators, and on the office door of a librarian on the main floor

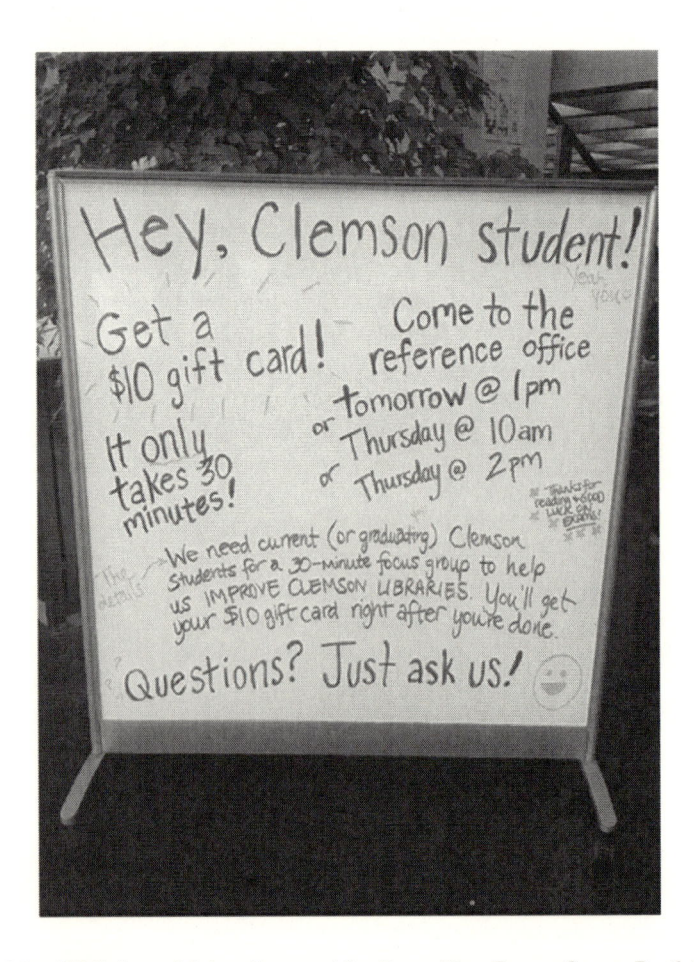

Figure 3.2. Whiteboard Advertisement for Recruiting Focus Group Participants.
Photo by Micki Reid

of the library. Immediately prior to each session, we placed a whiteboard with session information outside where the session would be held with an arrow directing students into the room and a clear indication of the incentive offered. Since we had an ample supply of library-branded marketing items such as can cozies, bookmarks, pens, and candy packets, we offered them freely to students at the start of each session.

Attendance increased with each session, which is logical since recruitment began less than forty-eight hours before the first session and exposure would have increased with each session held. The first session, held on a Wednesday afternoon, had two participants. The next session, held on Thursday morning at 10 a.m., had five. For our final session, we were incredibly fortunate to have eight attendees and distribute all available incentives without having to turn anyone away. While the session was a success, we do not endorse having one staffer host and record data for an unexpectedly large group of participants (in a small area).

The demographic breakdown of participants was also a pleasant surprise, as males and females were represented six to seven and there was at least one participant at each year of study from freshman to graduate student. Overall, students were responsive and appeared to provide honest and thoughtful feedback. As might be expected, individual expression and group size seemed to be inversely proportional. Students appeared satisfied with the formal study incentive and some seemed pleased about the additional free items we had available. While we did not formally solicit feedback about the timing of the focus groups, two students volunteered that they had already completed exams but returned to the library for the study. Other students still had exams to take but seemed to appreciate a brief, productive distraction. Examples of some of the information gathered can be seen in appendix 2. Information gathered in these sessions was used to improve both marketing and instruction in the libraries, with specific questions related to online instruction and learning objects.

Acquiring faculty feedback can prove to be difficult. Fortunately, it is possible to start a campus-wide initiative to begin conversations about research needs. This can take the form of a summit where invited faculty can mix with library faculty and staff to discuss specific, preselected topics. Clemson Libraries solicited feedback from campus constituents with summit meetings held in 2000, 2003, and 2006, and again in 2011. The first series of summits during 2000–2006 were designed to facilitate conversation about library issues to be used as a basis for the libraries strategic planning, discuss LibQUAL+ results, and, in 2006, to introduce the new dean of libraries and renew conversations about the libraries on campus.[1] During these summits, tables were assigned to seat both university and library representatives to discuss topics such as collection development, library services, and future directions. Notes were taken by library representatives and collected for consideration. In 2010, the Clemson Libraries changed its Federal Depository Library status from a shared regional to a selective depository. In 2011, the government documents librarian called a summit to gather stakeholders to discuss the federal documents collection and how this new status would affect its holdings. In addition to these kinds of hosted group meetings, librarians have the opportunity to attend departmental faculty meetings and can use this time to ask a select few questions and facilitate a mini–focus group to gather relevant information about awareness of library services or willingness to utilize online versus face-to-face library instruction tools. These kinds of opportunities for wider conversations about the library and its services and resources can catalyze internal discussions about changes in library instructional programming.

ONE-ON-ONE

While working with groups can undoubtedly produce useful feedback, some of the most candid feedback from faculty members often comes from more individualized interactions. One way to engage with faculty in a one-on-one setting is to create a program through the library that recognizes faculty research. Here at Clemson, we created the Researcher of the Month program wherein the library highlights a faculty member, staff member, or student by creating a poster, blog entry, or other public display that lists publications produced, classes taught, and other fun facts about the individual. While the honor is monthly, we limit it to months during the regular fall and spring semesters so recipients can receive the maximum amount of exposure possible.

The library can then follow up with the recipient by setting up a time to meet with them and hand-deliver a selected library promotional item such as a mug or imprinted folio. By scheduling this individual meeting, the library representative has the opportunity to ask how the library is meeting the research needs in the recipient's area(s) of expertise. For institutions with library subject specialists, having the liaison librarian conduct this visit can draw upon and bolster existing relationships. However, if you wanted to solicit feedback specifically about satisfaction with the subject liaison relationship, a new face might be a better choice since this would be a neutral party to ask those questions. Regardless of the personnel available, it is crucial to create a safe environment in which the recipient feels free to speak honestly about experiences and impressions, whether positive or negative. They should be assured that any information shared will be used for service improvement and never shared publicly or with their departmental colleagues. The library representative must work to be encouraging and avoid appearing judgmental. While it may be difficult to share, even a negative anecdote or admission of dis-

> Clemson Libraries > News & Events > Researcher of the Month Program

Researcher of the Month Program

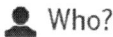

👤 Who?
A current student, faculty, or staff member that has contributed to the academic and intellectual culture here at Clemson University

🏆 What?
An opportunity to receive some recognition, gratitude, publicity for your research and projects, and some special library goodies

📅 When?
Each month during the spring and fall sessions, we will recognize one Researcher of the Month.

📍 Where?
We'll sing your praises (in poster format) in the lobbies of Cooper Library, Tillman Media Center, Gunnin Architecture Library in Lee Hall, and Special Collections. We'd also like to sing them virtually on our social media outlets.

💜 Why?
We love and appreciate our library users and want to recognize the amazing ways you are contributing to intellectual life here at Clemson.

😀 How?
We're on the lookout for people making a difference, but you can also nominate someone for recognition!

Figure 3.3. Researcher of the Month Webpage

interest in the library can provide valuable information for improving the user experience. Some questions to ask in this meeting might include

- What has the library done well for you in regard to your research?
- What has the library done well for your students?
- Name one service offered by the library that you have found to be very useful.
- Have you had a conversation about the library or library resources with a colleague lately? If so, what was the topic of discussion?
- How could the library do a better job of supporting your research?
- What library service do you think could be improved and how?
- How would you like to hear about what the library is doing to improve the research environment on campus?

You may also want to include questions to gauge awareness of specific services or resources. By asking, you will not only get feedback on the topic but also surreptitiously inform an unaware faculty member that it exists. For more ideas about questions to ask, see chapter 8. Taking the time to meet with constituents one-on-one can often produce feedback that is essential to the improvement of library services. For example, in one such meeting at Clemson University a faculty member suggested the possibility of adding a box on the interlibrary loan request form to ask that an item be purchased for the collection. Another meeting produced the idea of creating an "easy button" that would allow library patrons simply to make a request for a book without having to decide first whether they must request the book from interlibrary loan, our local consortial arrangement, or some other means.

ONLINE FEEDBACK FORMS

Creating opportunities for students and faculty to provide input on specific pieces of library instruction presents another possibility for instructional feedback. An article from 2012 describes the changes made to tutorial design based on feedback from twenty-one students with diverse backgrounds and learning styles.[2] Another study examined the effectiveness of interactive tutorials in an academic medical center and concluded that the online pieces they provided offered new ways for librarians to reach students with whom they may not ordinarily have come into contact.[3] Anonymous feedback forms can be valuable when collecting data about library instruction preferences. Even single-question surveys on virtual interfaces such as LibGuides can provide some insight into whether patrons prefer online, self-paced tutorials, or face-to-face instruction. There is also the opportunity to solicit suggestions for instruction topics of interest by providing a selection list or free-text entry field. Keep in mind that each free-text response field will add an additional level of resource investment for interpreting and categorizing the open-ended responses. That free-text field alongside your "other" option will garner at least one response that was covered by the choices you offered. Depending on the mood and maturity level of your respondents, you will also have at least one response that makes you wonder why someone would waste their time typing it. If you are tasked with processing feedback on something in which you have invested considerable time and energy, prepare yourself. Each time we survey undergraduates for feedback on one of our instruction programs, we receive at least one response that ranges from laughably irrelevant ("needs more cowbell") to stingingly candid ("they suck"). For libraries with the adequate survey and design resources, adding conditional logic can allow you to increase the relevance of questions and avoid overwhelming respondents with irrelevant fields or questions. Those librarians embedded in courses can request that their teaching faculty encourage students to fill out surveys.

With the cooperation of the instructor, the library survey could be emailed to students or made available within the course area of learning management systems, such as Blackboard and Canvas. The form can be as easy and brief as one or two questions:

Do you prefer learning about how the library can help you with your research . . .

    a. in brief face-to-face sessions (15 minutes or less)
    b. in more extensive face-to-face sessions (50+ minutes)
    c. in a brief (2 minutes or less) self-paced tutorial on a specific topic

What do you need to know more about to improve your research skills? (Select any that apply.)

    a. Citing sources
    b. Locating sources
    c. Evaluating sources
    d. Organizing sources
    e. Other:

If the survey is deployed outside of a specific class, it is a good idea to ask the status of the participant so that it is clear whether the respondent is a student or faculty or staff member. This knowledge will help you identify groups that need further assessment and can assist with the development of marketing campaigns once instruction items have been created and made accessible. For a more in-depth discussion of survey design and an overview of some specific survey tools, see chapter 9.

Another thought to consider is to turn the library's attention to groups on and off campus that have the potential to benefit greatly from library instruction but may sometimes be overlooked. For example, land grant institutions typically have agricultural extension agents who not only need ready access to library resources quite literally "in the field" but who also tend to collect large amounts of data that needs to be stored and made accessible. Both of these needs can be met by libraries via library instruction pieces. The library can begin to gather feedback about extension agent needs by sending out a survey that might include questions like those in appendix 3. Additional feedback and ideas can be gathered from some face-to-face time with extension agents during a "library road show" where librarians go to visit agricultural experiment stations and personally speak with those involved in field research about their needs and the possibilities for offering instruction from the library. Of course, this is a resource-intensive approach that would require available personnel, travel expenditures, and one or more significant blocks of work time.

Another group on campus that may offer valuable information for the library is the international student population. By working closely with student services and international student offices, the library can seek to identify opportunities for actively supporting international student communities. It is important to understand the cultural differences that may exist when offering library services to diverse populations since the library services provided at institutions in the United States may vary drastically from those offered in other countries. Therefore, some international students may not even think to ask a librarian for assistance while others may have high expectations that end in disappointment. While these mindsets are very different, they share the same potential detriment to users' library experiences. Yet, no matter the audience, gathering feedback from those whom we support is crucial. While there are a variety of effective forms for gathering this kind of data, we have had a good return on investment from and continue to use all the methods discussed in this chapter in combination to stay current on the needs of our students, teaching faculty, and campus community.

NOTES

1. "The Library Summit: Now that you have LibQual Survey Data, What will you do with it?," *LibQUAL+*, Feb. 7, 2008, http://www.libqual.org/documents/admin/Library%20Summit%20brochure.pdf.

2. Lori S. Mestre, "Student Preference for Tutorial Design," *Reference Services Review* 40, no. 2 (2012): 269.

3. Teresa L. Hartman and Alissa V. Fial, "Creating Interactive Online Instruction: The McGoogan Library Experience," *Medical Reference Services Quarterly* 34, no. 4 (2015): 415.

FOUR
Creating the Synchronous Workshop

Now that information has been gathered and decisions have been made as to what sessions will be offered, it is time to begin planning the online workshops. As with the preassessment phase, it is important to have a plan before getting started so that the larger picture is in focus. That makes planning the details much easier such as deciding which of the available online technologies will work best for your instructors, gathering ideas for engaging students in the online classroom, and deciding how (or if you want to) manage the recordings of live sessions. In this chapter, we will discuss these details and provide you with some ideas for your own programming.

CHOOSING AN ONLINE CLASSROOM TECHNOLOGY

To conduct a live online instruction session, you first must have a virtual space that can handle the delivery of your audio and possibly even video presentation as well as a way to communicate with your audience in real time. Most universities in the United States already offer at least one online course, so it is likely that your institution already has virtual classroom technology.[1] If so, it is highly recommended that you take advantage of it so that if you run into any problems you have support. If your institution has an employee or department dedicated to online education, this would be an excellent place to start asking about such technologies. For example, at Clemson our computing and information technology (CCIT) department had already chosen to work with Adobe Connect so we knew that would be a good place for us to start, knowing that before implementing a technology, Clemson should have performed its due diligence in researching its features, including accessibility compliance. By choosing an already supported technology, your institution should then be able to provide technical support either in-house or through its vendor or host after it is implemented. At Clemson, our CCIT department even provides a website with informational materials and instructions or scheduled, in-person assistance with Adobe Connect. Using the institution-provided classroom technology has the potential to benefit your students because using a technology that students are already familiar with will hopefully enable them to ignore its specifics and focus on the content being delivered. These students should also have already tackled any technological changes necessary, such as installing a required plug-in or fine-tuning audio levels. Based on the number of attendees, formality of the session, and availability of other types of instructor assistance, you may want to ask whether students familiar with the online classroom would volunteer to help their peers, if necessary.

Some institutions host online classrooms through a learning management system (LMS), such as Blackboard Collaborate but also provide online meeting spaces through accounts with services such as GoToMeeting or WebEx. If your institution happens to offer more than one technology that would work for hosting synchronous instruction, you now face the burden of choice in selecting the best option for your library's needs. If your institution does not provide or recommend any online classroom technology, you are in a similar predicament and must choose from among all the available options. Here are some considerations to investigate as you search for or compare options.

How much can (and will) your department or library spend for this technology? Unfortunately, this is the most practical place to start as it usually takes precedence over other considerations. If the answer happens to be a resounding "nothing," your field of choices has just narrowed considerably to include only those with free versions. Since the landscape of information technology providers changes rapidly, today's recommendations may be tomorrow's historical footnotes. Therefore, it is worth doing your own research into free webinar, meeting, and classroom technology. With that caveat and the proclamation that we by no means endorse any particular solution (paid or otherwise), below are three no-cost options with which you may want to begin your research:

- Google Hangouts
- join.me
- TeamViewer

It is worth noting that both join.me and TeamViewer offer paid versions as well as their free ones. Should you pilot and have excellent experiences and participation rates with one of those, you would have a convincing basis to use when you petition higher-ups for the funds to upgrade. We will not cover other purchase- or subscription-based meeting–hosting technologies because we have experience only with Adobe Connect and covering those options adequately would be outside of the scope of this book. The good news is that if you have a budget available for purchasing a technology, the potential companies should be forthcoming with information about their products' benefits and the ways they meet the specific pedagogical, technological, and accessibility needs of your institution.

Do instructors or students more commonly use one technology at your institution? Even if there is not a definitive institution-provided solution for online classrooms, it is likely that some of your colleagues, teaching faculty, and students have still had some experience with one. Reach out to them individually in a short survey to find out what technology they have used before and whether they would recommend it.

Does your institution already have a relationship with a company that provides this type of technology? Not surprisingly, the biggest names in online meeting technology are subsidiary products of some of the biggest names in general information technology services. Adobe offers several versions of its Connect technology, each with different meeting capacities, prices, and sets of features. Citrix and Cisco are the names behind GoToMeeting and WebEx, respectively. If your library or institution already has a business relationship with one of these vendors, it should not hurt to ask whether you could add online meeting technology at a discounted trial or bundle rate.

What are the technical capabilities, requirements, and limitations? At a minimum, the technology should allow one presenter to broadcast audio and visual elements live to multiple attendees. You should find out as many details about each of these aspects as possible before you decide whether to use the technology. Technical limits and your subscription or license determine the number of attendees allowed and the ways they are able to interact with you. Some technologies support multiple presenters and allow you to assign and retract presenter permissions for participants. Here are some important questions to answer as you evaluate a product for adoption or as you familiarize yourself with your institution-provided technology:

- Can the presenter upload and present from slides? Share their computer screen? Use a webcam or other video input?
- Can attendees interact with the host? With other attendees?
- What are the minimum requirements for processor and connection speed?
- Are any operating systems or web browsers excluded?
- Can you attend from a mobile device? Interact? Present?
- Can you record a session? If so, what can you do with the recording? Edit? Download? Caption?
- Are the URL and other connection specifics unique for each session or are they classroom-based so that you know that you are sending

a link that takes students directly into the classroom environment instead of to a product home page?
- How much effort is required for your audience members? Do they have to create an account? Download software or a plug-in?
- Does it support those who may have disabilities with features like keyboard-only access? Screen readers? Are any features specifically designed to include participants with auditory or visual disabilities? Could any be used that way?

You must consider connection speed requirements both for the presenter and for the attendee. If everyone will be using wired Internet from your institution, chances are you do not need to worry about the speed or quality. However, once you or your attendees venture onto wireless access or off campus, these become serious considerations. Your home Internet may be fast enough for email and watching YouTube videos, but is it strong enough to handle broadcasting images, audio, and video without lag? All the above questions are important to keep in mind as you enlist participants, since restrictions about permissions and technology types may need to be communicated to them before they even enter the virtual classroom.

PLANNING YOUR CONTENT AND DELIVERY

Now that you know which technology you will use and what exactly it can do, you must decide what to communicate in your online classroom and how to go about it. Audio is an expected part of this experience and there is a standard expectation that the presentation will be spoken with clarity at a reasonable speed and volume. In the unlikely event you are compelled to sing (or quote poetry), you are on your own as you deal with the added headaches of volume modulation and public performance rights. A basic set of headphones with an attached adjustable microphone is all you really need for webinar-quality audio. You should be able to obtain a model that more than meets your needs at a local or online store for fifty dollars or less. You may want to ask around or search online to compare your options. It is worth noting that some units may work well on one computer but not on another with a different configuration or operating system. We found this out the hard way once when, midway through a live session, our Mac-using presenter began to sound like a robot in a bee swarm.

Technology problems aside, the biggest determinant of audio quality is you. Speaking clearly requires pacing yourself, enunciating, and taming your otherwise beautiful and charming accent. As you become comfortable talking to your invisible audience and navigating the online classroom, your speech should become more natural and less rushed with fewer awkward pauses, nervous laughs, or newly developed vocal tics. When preparing content for a diverse audience of library neophytes, you should only use abbreviations, technical terms, and jargon with purpose and explanation. Idioms and regionalisms can also be problematic to students from other parts of the United States or for whom English is not their first language. You must remember that your audience sees and hears exactly and only what you are currently sharing with them. It may sound absurd but can be easy to forget that fact occasionally, especially when faced with nerves about a new form of public speaking. Remember to forewarn your students of extended audio pauses. While you may be perfectly aware that you have briefly muted your microphone to remove the cellophane from a new packet of sticky notes, your audience members are plunged into silence to ponder whether there has been a technical error on their end, for their instructor, or within the entire room.

Your environment is another aspect of audio quality that is largely within your control, aside from the odd fire alarm or impromptu construction project. Take note of any ambient noise where you plan to present and whether it is constant or intermittent. Constant noise can often be overcome with noise cancellation by the classroom technology or even your microphone. Silence your cell phone and your office phone. Put a sign on your door to let visitors know you are broadcasting. If someone might need to come in while you are talking, go ahead and unlock your door or leave it slightly ajar so you are not interrupted mid-sentence.

Depending on the nimbleness of your technology (and instructor), you will likely want to employ multiple methods for presenting visual content. Even in our fifteen-minute "Find It Fast" sessions, we combine slide presentation, screen sharing, and a limited amount of chat interaction. Below are some commonly supported content types and some considerations for their use.

Slides

Perhaps the biggest benefit to slides is the amount of control they give you over the presentation content. First, you can map out all your visual content in advance. You could provide screen shots of a website or database and not have to worry whether it happens to be working well at the moment you present. This means you can portion an appropriate amount of content per slide and add visual elements that reinforce your points. In case you have never attended a terrible presentation to learn this first-hand, we must insist that you do not put everything you plan to say on the slides. On a similar note, do not make your audience read one thing from the slides while you talk about something important yet unrelated. Slides are for reinforcing the main ideas of your presentation and for showing visual elements that enhance or elucidate your points. Second, the action of changing slides can help you maintain awareness of your pacing and how you are doing in relation to the total time you have available. Third, preparing slides means you can easily provide content to participants in advance or after the fact. For motivated audience members, getting slides in advance can help them approximate a flipped classroom since they can explore the content before ever "setting foot" inside the virtual space. Some students might choose to print the slides on their own and use them as a basis for note taking. Students with cognitive impairment can also benefit from having slides available in advance. If you are going to make slides available after the session, let students know this at the beginning. That knowledge will allow them to focus on processing and interacting with the content, especially the visual elements, rather than attempting to take detailed notes on or transcribe the entirety of the session. If you are using slides and fortunate enough to have more than fifteen minutes for your online session, the file is likely to be of a considerable size. Keep this in mind when preparing for the session and make sure you leave sufficient time to upload the slides to the classroom before it is time to greet your guests. When sharing your slides with students, file size and file type are both important considerations. If emailing your slides, keep in mind that many email clients have an upper limit for attachment size. If you are providing them at a download location, keep the file as small as possible while still maintaining what you think is the necessary level of visual integrity. Unless the newest version of Microsoft Office is required or provided by your institution, do not provide only a .PPTX file and assume your students can open it. A PDF file is probably your best option for inclusivity; however, you should take care to create a final product that is accessible to users with disabilities. If using Microsoft PowerPoint for your slides, versions from 2010 and forward provide a built-in accessibility checker.[2]

Screen Sharing

Live screen sharing is like being at the reference desk and turning the monitor around so the person you are helping can see exactly what you see and how you got to it. You can provide this personal, guided tour of a website or program despite the fact that you have more students than could ever crowd around one service desk. If you are going to present from your office or home computer, take a moment to walk through your process and pay attention to what additional things students could see. Whether you are sharing a particular program or your entire screen, you are likely to encounter some customizations that you may not particularly want broadcast to students. While there is no shame in conveying the sense that you are a genuine human, it can be easy to overshare accidentally with cookie-based browsing and information automatically saved by browsers. Does your web browser display your favorite sites at the top or when you open a new tab? Are you going to encounter any fields or forms where autofill might give away your personal information? Do any customizations change the experience from that of the typical user? One example of this would be an ad blocking browser extension, which can make it easy to forget that many free service websites and some YouTube videos have advertisements. Another example is that presenting from on campus means you may have seamless access to resources that could require proxy log in for students that are off-campus or even on campus via wireless Internet. One easy method of keeping your personal and instructional identities separate is to reserve one web browser for screen sharing and online presentations. If you generally use Chrome, Firefox should be clear of cookies. If you really want to appear industrious, you can have a favorites bar full of strictly professional links such as your library's homepage and your favorite citation manager. If you are going to share your entire screen, your desktop should be reasonably presentable and professional. Depending on your campus culture and personal interest in privacy, it may be just fine to leave your goofy family photo as your wallpaper. If your desktop is your go-to file depository, that can be distracting (never mind also ill advised); a quick fix is to put all the extra icons in a folder until you have finished your session. A computer with two screens is a wonderful resource for online instructors, especially those who will be presenting via screen sharing. This set-up allows you to dedicate one monitor to the content being shared while still being able to view the meeting room and/or your own digital outline and notes.

Instructor Video

Many online meeting and classroom technologies provide the option for the host to present a live video feed, generally from a webcam. Including webcam video has some definite potential benefits. It can foster and strengthen an interpersonal connection with your students despite disparate locations and possibly even time zones. Video helps to convey nonverbal communication and can be especially useful if the presenter is particularly expressive and engaging or if there are those in the audience that would use lip reading to aid comprehension of the verbal content. In accommodating attendees with hearing impairments, the video feed could actually be of a simultaneous sign language interpreter instead of the presenter. Unfortunately, the possibility of live video can be a discouraging factor for those otherwise eager to lead online instruction. When soliciting volunteers to lead online workshops, you may need to assure them that a live video feed of their face is not the focus of the session. One of the pluses of online interaction is the ability to attend sessions while eating, drinking, or wearing pajamas. The mere mention of a webcam has the power to rip away the good feelings that come along with this partial anonymity. Even a seasoned face-to-face instructor may hesitate or become self-conscious since the webcam view is far more concentrated than that of the average in-person student. The webcam can also detract attention from the content, especially if a lag develops between the audio and webcam feed. Since the content is the star, a video feed beyond the initial introduction should take up a modest portion of the total visual classroom space. Using a video feed increases the minimum need for connection speed and quality on both the presenter and audience sides. In the end, the decision whether to appear on camera should be up to the instructor. If you do choose to use a webcam, be sure to arrange a space that is not distracting and has adequate lighting. Familiarize yourself with the camera angle and field width beforehand so you can avoid presenting from up your nose or with only half your face. In most cases, webcam use should be limited to a brief personal introduction at the beginning of the session. Obviously, this will take time from the subject matter, so you need to decide if it is worthwhile based on the audience and the total length of time available to students.

Student Participation

Most online classroom technologies offer more than one method for students to provide feedback to the instructor. Beyond which methods are actually available, the length of your session and your instruction goals will be the biggest determinants of the quantity and type of participation you incorporate. Unless you somehow determine ahead of time that all of your audience members are adept at using all your offered feedback methods, you must sacrifice some of your instruction time at the beginning to provide a basic introduction to them. It is likely that during shorter or one-shot instruction sessions there will be a noticeable percentage of students who will not use any feedback mechanism, even despite your most flawlessly straightforward and engaging introduction to them.

Status Indicators

Usually displayed as icons, status indicators are a simple way for participants to convey information to the instructor and other participants. They are generally binary, one-at-a-time options that may be toggled on and off with a click of the mouse. Some status indicators remain in place indefinitely until cleared by the participant or instructor and others remain in effect for a limited amount of time. The "away" indicator is a common one due to its practicality and should be familiar to anyone with experience in AOL Instant Messenger or a similar one-on-one live chat platform. If your online sessions are less than an hour in length, you will probably not use the status indicator much; however, we have found it useful to enable it when you are logged in before a session but busy uploading slides or completing other in-room preparatory work.

Since our online instruction at Clemson Libraries takes place in Adobe Connect, status indicators are available to all participants. We encourage their use above other forms of interaction because instruction on them is quick and easy and students can use them without calling as much attention to themselves as they would with other input methods. We incorporate a basic introduction to status indicators, specifically the "agree" indicator, within our audio verification slide. Despite our prompt, we still generally encounter at least one participant per session that fails to use the status indicator. This prompts us to ask them verbally to indicate by status indicator or within chat if they can hear us. Since they would not hear this prompt if they were actually having audio difficulties, we would then follow that up with a private chat message if there were still no indication from the student. Binary status indicators such as yes/no and agree/disagree are useful as an on-the-fly polling method. During longer sessions, you can reconnect with your audience and refocus their attention by pausing occasionally to ask if they have prior experience with a topic or feel like they understand what you have covered so far. Students that fail to respond have now given you the opportunity to reach out to them directly and address any questions or technical difficulties.

Chat

Usually available in a dedicated content box or area, the chat feature is largely self-explanatory and is a great option for students that enjoy multitasking. Of course, it also requires a multitasking instructor as you must devote some attention to keeping up with it if you make it available and do not tell students otherwise. If you have expectations for how the chat is to be used, you should make those clear at the beginning of the session. You may choose to let your students know that you will check the chat occasionally and they should private chat you only with any pressing technical concerns. While you probably will not need to devote time in advance to it, you may occasionally need to remind students that chat should be reserved for discussing the topic at hand and should not distract them from it. In familiarizing yourself with the online classroom, it is worthwhile to take a moment and learn the quickest method for clearing or hiding the chat box. Although rare, it is not unheard of that a stray private chat be posted accidentally to all participants. This may be student-to-student commentary about you the instructor or some personal information (e.g., an email address, student ID number) that was intended only for you. Even if you do not want to use chat for interaction, it can be beneficial for conveying or clarifying content on the fly. Are you going to use a new word or one that might be unfamiliar to students?

Figure 4.1. Audio Test Slide

Type it in the chat. Giving a web address or bit of information that would be much easier to convey accurately in written form? The chat is a perfect place for it. Depending on the classroom technology, links typed in chat may automatically become active, allowing users (generally those on desktops or other large-format displays) the option of opening the webpage and following along with you or bookmarking it for later. Students would also be able to copy and paste information from the chat should they be taking their own digital notes while you talk.

Polls

Usually available in a dedicated content box or area, the polling feature allows you to display a prompt and its response options to your participants. You may choose to display the results to the room or keep them for your private use. Poll results are generally aggregated and anonymous, which makes them a good way to help the audience feel connected to other students without spotlighting or embarrassing any particular participant. If you have a very small audience, you should take an extra second to decide whether to display the results since a small sample size means it can be tempting and quite easy to determine who provided which answer. To make best use of classroom time, any polls to be used during the session should be created in advance. If you wanted to conduct an impromptu poll, it would be better to ask the question aloud and ask participants to respond with a status indicator or in chat. You should get in the habit of mentioning the poll verbally both to let your students know you would now like their input and to enable them to let you know if they cannot see or interact with it. Depending on the technology, your poll may require an additional step to open it once it is already displayed; this can occasionally be overlooked, so it can be helpful to let students know they should be able to see the poll as well as give their response. Polling at the beginning of a session is a great way to introduce participants to the interactivity of the online environment while also getting some baseline data about your audience. For example, you could begin an Introduction to Google Scholar session with the following poll:

How often do you use Google Scholar?

- Never
- I have before but do not currently
- Occasionally
- Once a month
- Once a week or more
- Other: type your answer in chat

You should be open to adjusting your content coverage based on poll results, adding a bit more background if no one has ever used it or skipping the basics if you somehow managed to populate the audience of your "introductory" class with a group of experienced users. While polling is great for informing the session itself, it can also be put to work as a source of more formal assessment data. For instruction planning, it can be helpful to know whether attendees are faculty, staff, or students or at which year of study are your student attendees. If you do not collect demographic data during session registration, you have the option to request it with a poll. Since polls are generally session specific, you would need to transfer the responses to a dedicated spreadsheet or other collection mechanism before you leave the classroom.

Question and Answer (Q&A) Boxes

If you provide a chat box, also providing a Q&A area may seem redundant. However, there are a few reasons you may want to devote some classroom space to displaying it temporarily or throughout the session. Having students use the dedicated Q&A box means you can collect questions and address them at regular intervals or at the end. Keeping track of questions that occur within chat can be demanding, especially when participants also use the chat box to interact with each other. It can be empowering and aid learning when one student answers another. However, it can also mean that you miss an opportunity to address something that would benefit multiple students or, in the worst-case scenario, have a student leave your session satisfied with an incomplete or incorrect answer from another attendee. Since Q&A boxes allow anonymous questions, they can also provide a safe place for attendees to ask without the fear of embarrassment.

Collaboration and Presentation

While student collaboration can be achieved for small audiences verbally or within chat, you may wish to incorporate a group activity using an available collaboration feature. A collaborative activity can allow your students to synthesize content, learn while doing, and reinforce knowledge gained by sharing it with their peers. Unfortunately, it requires advanced planning and instruction time. It also relies on the willingness of the instructor to relinquish control of the session, if only briefly or partially, and the good fortune to have recruited attendees who are both willing and able to follow your instructions. Two common features that enable collaboration are the whiteboard and the subclassroom space, which we will refer to as a "breakout" room. Of these two, the whiteboard requires the least in terms of power relinquishment and student obedience. The whiteboard provides a blank space on which the instructor and students can simultaneously place text and images. Depending on participants' connection speeds and the amount of data on the whiteboard, a lag time can sometimes occur between the creation and display of content items. This can occasionally mean one user inadvertently posts content that overlaps with or covers someone else's.

Breakout rooms require advanced setup in their creation and explicit instructions to students on their intended function. More important, using breakout rooms requires students that can follow your directions in selecting, joining, and interacting within their designated rooms as well as returning to the main classroom at the specified time. Once you turn students loose to their rooms, you should be ready to help those that cannot follow the directions you just gave. You should also accept the fact that one or several students may have disappeared altogether.

TO RECORD OR NOT TO RECORD

If your technology allows you to record the session, you have even more decisions to make before you present! You may decide not to record since this has the potential to add an extra level of intimidation for both the instructor and the students. It can be especially stressful if the instructor begins to falter or there are technical or other difficulties. If you do choose to record, you should inform your audience about that at the beginning of each session and let them know the purpose and access level of the recording. Even if you choose to record only for internal quality assurance and training purposes, you should let them know what you are doing. For our instruction, we record the session and send an access link afterward only to the session participants. Given the restricted audience, we also do not have to allocate resources to captioning or transcribing these recordings since we have not yet had an attendee request this accommodation. Since all the recipients were there (at least briefly) during the session and the recording is hosted on our server, there is no additional concern about privacy. When designing online meeting spaces with recording functionality, most technology companies have already considered attendee privacy and included a method for preserving their anonymity such as by hiding the attendee list and chat box. Of course, this does not help if you or someone else audibly addresses a student by name. If you do choose to record sessions, you should put a file management plan in place before the first session begins. Some questions to help guide your planning:

- Where will recording files be stored? Are there any limitations on individual file size, video length, total storage capacity, and so forth?
- Is video publication automatic or does it require you to make a change in the classroom system?
- How soon after a session will its recording be made available? How will you let students know it is available?
- Are any student identifiers included in the recording? Is there any other reason it would need password protection?
- How long should students be able to access the recordings?
- Who is in charge of deactivating, archiving, and deleting recordings?
- Can you track accesses or views? If so, will you? How will you use this data?

Although you are likely to encounter on-demand help videos that are recorded from live sessions, we do not recommend making recordings publicly available in this way. One reason is that live instruction sessions with audience interaction will invariably include segments that are not necessary for later use. If you begin by instructing students on how to interact within the classroom, it is best to begin your recording and session introduction afterward. Regardless, most interactive instruction will also contain segments within the session that just are not necessary for later viewers. If you are adept with the options for editing a recording, it can seem reasonable to add time stamps at the beginning of content chunks or even try to edit out those pauses. Unless it was somehow the best instruction session that ever took place, your time would be much better spent preparing a recording that is specifically created for asynchronous use. Cutting twenty minutes of down time from the recording of your fifty-minute session is labor-intensive and still leaves the end user—someone that probably ended up at your video via Google search—facing a thirty-minute video for the two-minute tidbit of information they need.

Since we do not recommend having session recordings serve the purpose of publicly available instruction videos, we could delay any mention of captioning until our section on dedicated video tutorials. However, as representatives of a profession that exists to connect people with knowledge, we cannot resist this opportunity. Any video you make available to the public should have accurate captions. If you only have the technology for open captions, ones that always display during viewing, you may wish to make available captioned and noncaptioned versions. If you host your videos on YouTube, their automatic closed captioning gives you an excellent start; however, you must follow up to edit those captions for accuracy. If you were somehow able to create an instruction video yet are unable to take the last step and provide accurate captions, provide an accurate transcript and be prepared to defend your position that providing equal access would be an undue burden to your institution.

CREATING A COMFORTABLE ONLINE ENVIRONMENT

When a student attends a live online workshop, it is important not to take for granted the fact that they may have never been in that particular online space before. Unlike a physical classroom that contains many things that are nearly universally familiar to any student (desks, chairs, a door, windows, a lectern), the same is not necessarily true in the online environment. It is important to take just a moment of class time to introduce students to the space. Our solution for student orientation is to have all presenters use a standard set of introduction slides. The first slide, displayed before the session officially begins, lets students know there is audio playing and they should be able to hear it (fig. 4.1). It also provides an annotated screenshot excerpt that walks them through the process of how to use the room's technology to indicate whether they can hear the music. It also has an annotated screenshot on how to initiate the audio configuration sequence if they do not have audio. The next slide has the session title, branding title, and the photo, name, and title of the presenter(s) (fig. 4.2). Both of these slides have institutional branding and use fonts that are common on any machine. It is wonderful to use your institutionally approved fonts, but not if some of your presenters do not have them and will have to default to something that may or may not leave the content legible and well-spaced.

Creating the Synchronous Workshop 49

Advanced Google Searching

Anne Grant
Instruction Coordinator

Figure 4.2. Session Introduction Slide

It is a good idea to run through these basic steps to ensure that students are comfortable and have at least shared baseline knowledge of the online classroom environment. One of the most difficult parts of switching from the face-to-face environment to online is losing the ability to see the students' faces, which can make it hard to ascertain when they are getting something and when they need more help. A furrowed brow or a quizzical glance that an instructor might see from the corner of their eye in a traditional setting usually indicates this, but now all they get is silence and their computer screen. This silence can be somewhat unnerving. However, once the instructor realizes that this is a normal part of online teaching, it can make them more comfortable letting those silences happen when they are needed.

Technical difficulties can be one of the most challenging parts of teaching online and as anyone who has used computers will know, they are almost guaranteed to happen at some point. One way of avoiding problems is to make your instructions and expectations clear even to those with no prior online meeting experience. If you will be asking students to use the virtual whiteboard, make sure they all know how to do it by providing a brief overview of use and then maybe letting them try it. This can let them get their urge for artistic expression out of the way and should translate to fewer intentional or unintentional stray marks (or doodles of your school mascot). If students have microphone access that you cannot disable as the session administrator, make sure they know how to turn it off before they eat a bowl of cereal or call their significant other during your presentation. Being direct with your instructions and expectations can prevent a lot of on-the-fly problem solving and/or crisis management.

Bring a Buddy

When you are juggling presentation methods (audio, screen sharing, chat) and one or more feedback methods (status indicators, private chat, public chat), it can be easy to let a ball drop. Since you are perfectly aware of the content and still see it on your computer, you may not be aware that things are not going so well for your students. It may be that your audio is cutting out intermittently or the sound in the supplemental video you are playing is only coming through your own headphones. We may even know of someone who has switched off their office surge protector with their foot, effectively disappearing before their students' eyes and requiring several minutes to reboot. These are times when an instruction assistant is a lifesaver. Your assistant does not have to be an expert on your topic or the technology, just someone that is paying attention and quick to react. Their basic role is to make sure things are what they seem and communicate with you and/or your students should something odd happen. The ideal assistant is willing and able to jump into chat to paste a URL or answer a quick question and perhaps even take the microphone should yours happen to go mute. It may be that they private message you, text you, or rap gently on your office door to show you a hastily written sign to let you know that you sound like a robot being attacked by bees. Of course, the more added value your assistant can provide, the better. Have an experienced colleague willing to step up to the virtual lectern should you disappear? Excellent! However, any level of assistance can mean a dramatically better experience for your students, helping you smooth bumps along the way and end up with satisfied customers.

Assess the Situation

Use your student feedback mechanism to determine whether the problem is affecting one or multiple users. For single-user issues, ask the participant to log out of and log back into the online environment. This will often fix the problem. If they are still having issues, offer to send them documentation from the class later. For multiple-user issues, the first suggestion is still to have all those effected log out and log back into the class.

Do Not Panic!

It is crucial that you maintain a calm attitude. The occasional technical difficulty does not have to give you or your students a bad impression of online instruction. If troubleshooting and repair of the problem would take up too much of the session length, simply reschedule the class or offer to send out the slides along with your notes. Remember that technical difficulties are never the end of the world, just sometimes the end of the class for the day.

Taking these first steps into the online classroom can be overwhelming as you consider available technologies, student engagement, and recording options, but a little bit of planning and a thoughtful approach can make the process easier. Also, keep in mind that you need to consider both your library instructors and the students and faculty whom you are teaching as you plan these sessions. Make sure you are using tools and techniques that enhance and yet do not distract from your ultimate goal of relaying information literacy skills and valuable updates about library resources and services.

NOTES

1. Elaine I. Allen and Jeff Seaman, "Changing Course: Ten Years of Tracking Online Education in the United States," Babson Survey Research Group (2013): 21.

2. "Creating Accessible PowerPoint Presentations," *Microsoft*, accessed November 3, 2015, https://support.office.com/en-ca/article/Creating-accessible-PowerPoint-presentations-6f7772b2-2f33-4bd2-8ca7-dae3b2b3ef25.

FIVE
Moving from Workshop to Tutorial

We discussed recording live instruction sessions in the previous chapter, but we also did not recommend publishing that video for general use. This leaves us with the elephant in the room: how to provide workshop content for asynchronous use so that all those patrons who missed your amazing session or have a just-in-time need can benefit from your instructional efforts. While the term *tutorial* may be used to refer to both interactive and static learning objects, we will be using it in this book to refer to non-interactive instructional audiovisual recordings (videos). In this chapter, we will discuss broad concepts that must be considered when you create your tutorials; these considerations will drive later decisions on the kinds of software you choose as well as the ways that you are able to distribute your videos. We will also highlight the different types of videos that you could choose to create, another choice that will dictate later decisions about software and distribution. Finally, we will walk you through the creation of an online tutorial step-by-step so that you will be able to wrap your head around the entire process from start to finish.

GENERAL CONSIDERATIONS

Branding and Consistency

Just as the slides you use in your virtual classroom should reflect well on your institution, your videos should be a professional, appealing representation of the content. It is also important to create a quality product because tutorials have a longer life span than a live online presentation (except if recorded for repurposing as discussed below) and a large potential audience. When considering videos as a product, you should also plan for some consistency among the videos themselves. This does not mean you have to use the same format or speaker for each one; however, you should be prepared for how you might indicate that videos are sequential on a topic (e.g., beginner, intermediate, advanced) or deal with related concepts such as database search tutorials.

Technical Preparations

The first thing to remember as you sit down to record is that your computer should be prepared for screen capture footage just as it would be for screen sharing, as we discussed in-depth in the previous chapter. However, you may also want to go a step further and create generic "test" log-ins or accounts to be used within your video to prevent the accidental display of your personal information. Having your live audience see your email address or phone number in a one-time synchronous workshop is a bit different from having it available 24/7 in a public video. When we worked with our Interlibrary Loan office to make videos, we coordinated with them to get a test account that would not reflect any personal information and would also allow their staff to know those requests did not need to be processed or counted in statistics. For creating accounts in many other database or free web services, you could use your library's general email address or, depending on the video technology you use, do some creative editing to make it appear as if you have created a new account using a fake email address (e.g., tigerstudent@clemson.edu).

Intellectual Property and Copyright

Creating your own content means you get to consider the intellectual property of items within your creation *as well as* how you would like your creation to be used by others (if at all). Before you start searching for images or sound bites to use in your video, check whether your institution has a copyright policy that allows you to take advantage of Creative Commons licensing. If your institution reserves all rights to content created under its name, you will be unable to comply with the Creative Commons licenses with ShareAlike provisions (CC BY-SA 4.0 and CC BY-NC-SA 4.0).[1] In short, you would not be able to use content with these license types because you would technically be unable to fulfill the requirement that your product be used with that same freedom. When using copyrighted material, remember that an example or design element you use in your virtual classroom is not necessarily one you can reuse in a video tutorial. The elements of the four-factor test may be weighted differently if your video now makes that snippet of music or image available to the public at any time. If you use specialized software for creating your video, you should also be aware there might be stipulations for the program you use. Numerous video creation services are available free online, some for a time-limited trial period or only for educational use. The final video will often bear the watermark or logo of the product, which you should not even consider trimming or covering. If your institution or the type of content you have incorporated does not already dictate the copyright status of your video product, you must now decide how you will allow others to use it. By their essence, educational works are created for sharing knowledge. Therefore, you should at least consider publishing your video under some type of Creative Commons license.

Accessibility

At a minimum, you should fulfill any accessibility requirements set forth by your institution. If you are unfamiliar with the relevance of Section 508 and other regulations to your institution, there should be someone you can contact in Student Disability or Accessibility Services. The US General Services Administration provides information about Section 508 requirements as well as tools and checklists for creating compliant videos (and other files) on its website.[2] Just be warned that knowledge of accessibility standards brings with it the awkward uncertainty about what to do when encountering videos (perhaps even by your institution) that do not provide captions. Given the fact that video hosting with closed captioning is available free from YouTube, there is really no good excuse not to provide captions even if you are not required to do so.

CHOOSING A VIDEO TYPE

There are several major types of options for providing workshop content for public, asynchronous use. The method you choose will depend on the resources you have available in terms of time, technology, and skill. You will almost certainly use different methods depending on your evaluation of the immediacy of the need, the time you have available to invest in the project, and the content's potential longevity and audience.

Type 1: Video Created from an Archived Live Session

This type of tutorial involves removing as much unnecessary content as possible from the recording of a live workshop. We list this as the first option because it requires the least amount of additional effort to create a video. If the final product is created by or in consult with the original presenter, it can be easy to identify points to be removed. However, as we mentioned in the previous chapter, we do not recommend this option. That workshop was delivered in an environment far different from that of the asynchronous, solitary viewer and the content, tone, and general feeling are going to reflect that. Assuming you did not compromise the synchronous experience with a repurposed recording in mind, your workshop was interactive, personable, and had some energy or even spontaneity. While invaluable to the original participants, all of these interactions, pauses, and "try it yourself" times need stripping from the video. Unless you put additional effort into transitions and timing, these cuts will undoubtedly lead to some awkward lead-ins and pacing. Editing within a session recording may be a feature of your online classroom technology, but Adobe Connect only allows trimming at the beginning and end of a session. If your technology shares this limitation (or offers no editing capability), you would need to download the session recording to your local computer and have and use video editing software to modify it.

Type 2: Video Created as a Live Recording without an Audience

This method reuses all the intellectual effort you have put into your synchronous session. In its simplest form, this method means you distill your content—omitting the classroom orientation, interactive elements, and time-specific references—and perform it in an empty "room" while you record. One of the most difficult aspects of this method is you need to perform it reasonably well from beginning to end in one take. This is not an endeavor for the perfectionist. The longer your presentation, the greater your appreciation must be for the beauty of imperfection. Each minute seems to make the task exponentially more difficult as you are at the mercy of mental, vocal, technical, and environmental circumstances. You can prevent some stress during the presentation if you have and plan to use video editing capabilities; however, you must always remember to balance the equation, putting a reasonable amount of time and effort in based on the expected use, audience, and lifespan of the product.

Type 3: Video Created Using Specialized Software

Many companies specialize in the creation of visually attractive tutorials that can be relatively easy to use and range in both price and functionality. At Clemson, we have used a couple of different products and will explain two of these (VideoScribe and Adobe Captivate) in more detail later in this chapter. VideoScribe is a product that allows us to create engaging, animated videos after mastering a challenging technological learning curve; its current annual subscription is less than $200. VideoScribe is a web-based product whose current annual subscription for use is $144. There are other free options such as Prezi[3] and, if your institution has a site license for Microsoft, you can even use PowerPoint creatively. If you prefer to create a collection of images and short videos with a musical background, perhaps offering a tour of your library spaces, you might consider another web-based video production tool like Animoto for a small annual fee.[4]

STEP-BY-STEP GUIDE FOR CREATING YOUR TUTORIAL

There are many decisions to make before you start recording any audio or video. To make things even murkier, there are few definite answers about how to plan and present your content. We kept our workflow as relevant as possible for all types of tutorial creation. We will attempt to discuss the considerations for each of the major decision points in tutorial creation; however, these are only guidelines as you decide what will and will not fit your resources and needs.

Step 1: Outline, Script, or Storyboard

There should be no question *whether* to plan what you will cover, because this is a crucial component of your tutorial. The outline is the first step and depending on your needs, it may also be the last because when you create an outline, you determine the exact concepts you will

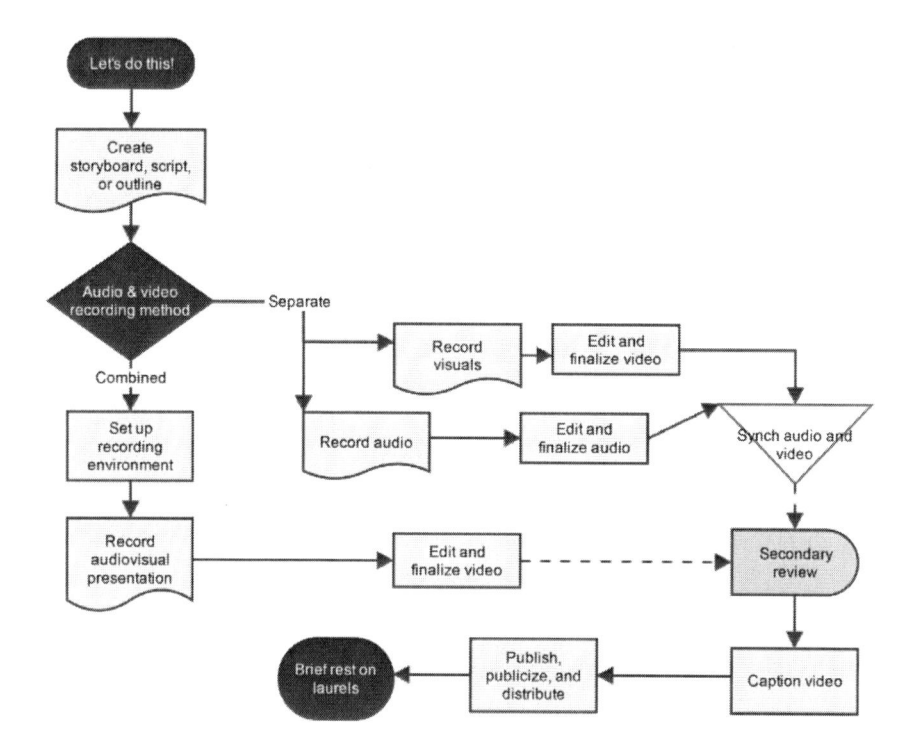

Figure 5.1. Sample Workflow for Creating a Tutorial Video

cover and lay out the order in which they will be presented. If you are not using the outline of an existing workshop, identifying an information need is a great place to start. Did you receive an instruction request for a particular topic or skill? Is there a recurring reference question that you could help answer? Is there a library task or process that a large number of your patrons will need to do? Once you know of a topic, outlining it will probably seem very familiar as a sort of combination of defining a research question and establishing learning outcomes. If you work in a larger library, you should not have to go it alone when mapping out content for a discipline-specific assignment or database as your subject specialists will be there to help you in your planning.

Creating an outline will allow you to establish exactly how much content you have in mind to cover, which can often be much more than you originally thought. For topics with instructions or processes, you need to make sure each step is addressed and you may want to take into account the environment(s) from which your video will be accessed. For example, when creating a video that will only be available and accessible from within a course management system, you may want to point viewers to library resources that are linked to within that space. For other videos with multiple or no specified access point, you will want to begin in a neutral location such as your library's website.

Once you have created a project outline, the uncertainty comes in when you decide whether this is enough. For those lucky few who are skilled in speaking extemporaneously while remaining on topic and avoiding pauses, an outline may suffice. However, we are in favor of writing a script for several reasons. First, having a script means you can review your content long before you go through the effort of creating a draft video. It is a good idea to have someone else review the script for clarity and accuracy. If this video is in collaboration with a subject specialist, it is a good idea to have them review it. If it is for a particular professor, they may be open to reviewing your script to make sure it is in line with their expectations. If there is no one available to help, take some time to step away from the document before you come back and review it with a relatively fresh perspective. For a video about library processes like searching a database, follow exactly what the words say and see if you achieve the result you want your viewers to get. Second, a script is an invaluable starting point when captioning your video. Your final audio will likely differ from your original script, but the majority of the transcription work will already be done. If you choose to host your video in YouTube, you can upload a script and have it set the timings automatically. Finally, a script provides a quick way to know almost exactly what you cover in your video without having to sit through it all to check. In that case, when (not if) your library undergoes a change in its resources, services, or policies, you can open the script file and perform a Ctrl-F (Command-F on Mac) and see whether the video needs updating by searching for keywords. For example, if your service points merged (as they did here at Clemson) and you need to change occurrences of "reference desk" with "library services desk," using this feature makes it easy to find in a written script.

The storyboard is the most detailed option to help you plan specifically what you will show while you speak. The most basic method is to create a two-column table. In the left-hand column, paste your script. In the right-hand column, describe in as much detail as you need what visuals will be displayed during that segment of audio. Add a new row in the table for each segment of audiovisual content until you reach the end of your script. While you may prefer to storyboard all your videos, we reserve it for videos in which there is no need for recorded web or software usage. This is generally the case for videos on more concept-based topics such as information evaluation or plagiarism. Below are a few more details to consider when creating your script or storyboard. If you plan to record your audio from just an outline, you may want to skip ahead and refer back to them just before you are going to record it.

- Consider whether to mention URLs, phone numbers, email addresses, and similar content. Unless you must designate an https prefix, do not subject your audience to hearing you slowly state, "H-T-T-P colon . . . " If you can access your site without the www, omit that as well. If you are going to create a separate, audio-described version of the video, you can briefly highlight the URL in the address bar area and avoid providing it verbally.
- If showing a website or database that can be accessed from a mobile device, keep in mind that it may look quite different to mobile users due to responsive design. For example, the boxes on a three-column LibGuide appear in one long column to mobile viewers. While you must decide how important this consideration is for your video content, it is worth noting that responsive design is popular practice among web designers and sites with mobile-friendly design receive an uptick in their Google results ranking. If you are not familiar with responsive design or would just like to see what happens on different devices, you can visit MobileTest.me, choose a device, and enter a URL.[5] Since item positions may change (and some students may not be able to see your video at all), it is best to avoid identifying an item only by its screen position. Mention the item exactly as it is named on the screen (shortening if necessary) and, if available, its location within a menu or under a heading. Instead of "Use the email link in the box at the top of the right-hand column," try "Use the 'Contact Us' link in the 'More Help' box." Similarly, do not distinguish an item only by its color such as, "Sources in the blue box are the ones you should try first" because screen display colors can vary and this information might be com-

pletely unhelpful for viewers with partial or complete colorblindness.
- Keep it moving. As mentioned previously in the section about retrofitting a session archive, your tutorial viewers do not want to sit through pauses. Most viewers of online videos understand they are able to pause, rewind, and rewatch on their own and do not want or need you to take a moment so they can "catch up." If you insist on reminding them, do it in the video description, not the video itself. To keep our videos quick, we even trim the time we spent typing information into search and form fields; unless you are pointing out something specific, no one needs to see each letter appear on the screen.

Step 2: Creating a Quality Audio Recording

When making a video, the temptation is to focus so much on the visual content that the audio does not receive due consideration. The first few seconds of a video are critical. Have you ever opened a help video only to be met with a long and boring introduction? Most college students will have been exposed to every sort of video presentation and will probably begin to abandon a video that takes more than two seconds to load, so it should be no surprise that a few seconds of poor-quality audiovisual content would be similarly off-putting.[6] Since there is only so much you can show in the first few seconds, we argue that the pacing and quality of the audio is what matters most in decreasing viewer abandonment.

Pacing

After analyzing "millions of data points" about video retention, Wistia (a blog about video marketing and production) offers the succinct but definitive advice that "shorter is better."[7] While the focus of their analysis was on "business video," there is no reason to think of our educational content as something that would be subject to drastically different outcomes. We might see a slightly higher retention rate due to the external motivation of academic success in the form of professors who require use of your videos, but we certainly cannot rely on it. You will want your audio to move quickly enough to maintain attention, but slowly enough to allow information to be absorbed. It is a balancing act as you consider elements that must be included versus those that might be trimmed to help focus on the main points of the video. For example, we want our viewers to feel a personal connection, so we like to introduce ourselves and communicate expected learning outcomes for each instruction object. Since our videos must be short and begin with strong content delivery, where can we put all this information? Instead of thinking of your video

Moving from Workshop to Tutorial 61

as equivalent to your online workshop, take into account the fact that it will exist within an online context. This environment will almost certainly be a place that allows you a space to provide this introductory information without bogging down your video and slowing your pace.

Quality

For many who are about to embark upon the audio recording journey, the type of microphone to buy is the number one consideration. While it is essential equipment, your microphone does not need to be anything expensive. Thus far, we have used a Logitech headset with microphone for all our online workshops and recordings. While you can certainly buy a desktop microphone and spend well above fifty dollars, you do not have to do it to get a respectable recording. We will cover a few simple things you can do as you record to ensure a good-quality product, but much of the rest can be fixed after you have spent a little time getting familiar with Audacity.

- Adjust your microphone. Just as you would perform an audio check before conducting an online session, test your volume level before you launch into a recording. Instead of just using the old,

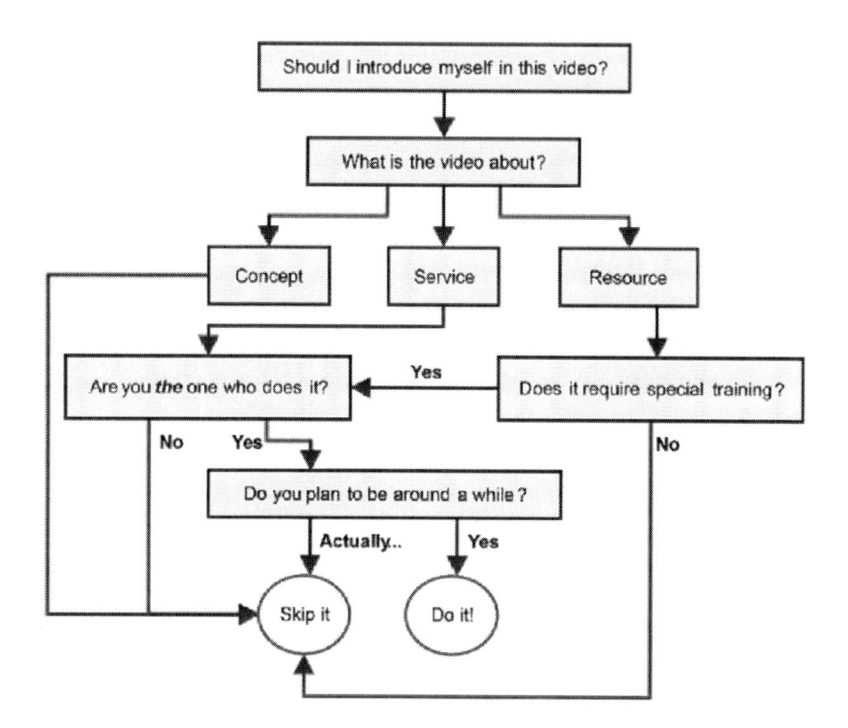

Figure 5.2. Video Introduction Decision Tree

"Testing 1-2-3," be sure to throw in something that starts with a "P." Trying out this sound, called a plosive, can help you know whether to move your microphone away from your face. If you find yourself unable to get clear audio without blowing out the range of your plosives, you may need a microphone you can use with a pop filter. As for the filter itself, you can buy one or Google instructions on how to make it yourself.
- Manage your environment. Just as for live workshop delivery, you will want to do what you can to remove distractions and disruptions. Silence the ringer on your phone(s), put a note on your door, and keep your feet well away from the power switch of your computer's surge protector.
- Talk like you mean it. Not every subject is going to be the most engaging ever, but your audience is depending on you to do what you can. Do everything you can to avoid sounding like you are reading from a script. All the technical quality in the world cannot compensate for a droning, monotone narrator. While you do not want to strain the extremes of your recording software, put some variation in your voice!

Most video creation programs provide the ability to record and edit narration as one of their multitude of features. If available, the audio editing options are generally limited since this is not the primary purpose of the software. While you could settle for what you can accomplish using this built-in feature and spend your time fiddling with any editing options, we highly recommend you consider the dedicated audio editing program Audacity.[8] This powerful program is free (open source) and has versions available for Windows, Mac, and Linux/GNU platforms. True to the spirit of open-source software, there are tutorials readily available and an extensive manual both included with full installation and available online.[9] With more than forty effects and ten file type options for exporting your completed project, Audacity has a depth of functionality that we have hardly explored and that may prove intimidating for some users. Therefore, we will focus on a few of the tasks we have found especially useful for fine-tuning our audio narration and creating a polished-sounding product with minimal difficulty. The first time you accidentally delete your entire audio track, just relax and press Ctrl-Z (or Command-Z on Mac)! Audacity responds to this and other keyboard shortcuts (e.g. Ctrl-X, Ctrl-V) that may now be hardwired in Windows or Microsoft Office users.

- Silence is golden. When recording, leave one or two seconds of silence at the beginning of your session (or end if you forget)—more on that in a moment. Since your microphone is probably not exactly where it was when you last recorded, adjust it just before each recording session. If you speak softly, you can likely amplify your recording satisfactorily in postproduction. The bigger danger is speaking too loudly for your setup. If you cannot see the full top and bottom of your loudest audio waves, they are being clipped. The data is being lost, sometimes irretrievably, but the fix is simple: not so loud! You may need to move the microphone farther from you, adjust the microphone input level, or just try to dial your voice back a notch. Remind yourself (or your subject if coaching someone else) that mistakes will happen. Just pause a second and begin the phrase or sentence again. Once you have your recording, the cut and paste functionality means no one will ever know you said *journicle* instead of *journal article*.

- Noise Removal. Click and drag to highlight those seconds of relative silence you left while recording and then go to Effects > Noise Removal. Under step 1, click the "Get Silence" button to analyze the segment you have selected. Click off your selection (select the entire track), open Noise Removal again, and press the OK button. The noticeability of this edit will depend on how noisy your background was during recording, but you will probably see that the pauses between your words got a little flatter as that background noise was removed.

- Adding extra silence. Once you have identified something that needs to be silenced or a segment without content that you would like perfectly quiet, highlight the segment and use one of the two methods for accomplishing this. You can choose Generate > Silence . . . from the toolbar and confirm with the OK button or use the button that shows a sound wave with a flat portion in the middle. Its tooltip is "Silence Audio" and it is located on the Audacity Tools toolbar beside the left-pointing arrow "Undo" button. The ability to add silence is a wonderful thing when you are faced with the startling reality of just how much noise your mouth makes when you are not technically speaking and just how loudly you breathe. Anywhere you want to keep your pause but not the noise within it, you can add silence. Performing this step after removing background noise will allow you to approximate the result of having recorded in a dead-silent recording studio. As you gain experience working with sound files, you will become able to recognize the waveform of actual speech in contrast with preceding mouth and intermittent breath noises or computer clicks. Keep in mind when adding silence between phrases that not every waveform that looks isolated is a stray sound. It can be especially easy to mistake the trailing "s" sound of a plural noun for stray noise.

Step 3: Creating Your Video

Many technology options are available to create audiovisual presentations—so many that covering the field thoroughly would be beyond the scope of this book. In lieu of attempting a broad overview of options that we have not used, we will discuss the two video creation programs with which we are most familiar. We use these programs to create very different types of videos, so they do at least introduce the spectrum of possibilities offered by desktop video creation software.

VideoScribe

A product of the company Sparkol, this program allows you to create engaging animated videos with whiteboard-style imagery. For those accustomed to creating visual presentations in PowerPoint, the learning curve can be very gradual. If you are not detail-oriented and meticulous, this software is likely not a good match for you. The options for types of visual elements include text, images from the provided library, and imported images. For each element, you must set aspects that include the manner in which it appears on the "canvas," how quickly it appears, and whether there is a pause afterward. The options for how an element should arrive include appear, move onto the screen, morph from an existing element, or be drawn or placed by your choice of writing utensils or hands. You can also import and incorporate your own images such as your library word mark or logo, screenshots, or stock photos. For an imported image to interact with the rest of the content like a native image, it must be formatted as a scalable vector graphics (SVG) file. While we often use one or more imported files within our "scribes," we have only used an SVG file once. Not being graphic designers, we located an existing free-to-use SVG image that was similar to what we had in mind for our video. Unfortunately, the vector graphics software provided by our institution (and thus most familiar to us) is Adobe Illustrator, which cannot open SVG files. Thus, we had to download and install Inkscape[10] so we could save the image as an Illustrator-compatible file and edit it. At this point, Illustrator's ability to export to (save as) SVG format was little consolation. Why exactly did we go to all that effort? The only way to ensure a borderless image for an imported file is to use an SVG and we wanted a mortarboard image that could land seamlessly atop the head of a figure, unencumbered by an opaque white background.

Of our four current videos created with VideoScribe, the shortest is thirty-eight seconds and the longest is one minute and forty-one seconds. They average a little more than one hundred image elements each with an average rate of 1.32 images per second. To be clear, each element may cause only a subtle change in the overall view or may exist simply to cover up other elements, effectively wiping clean or resetting part or all of the canvas. This inability to remove items from the canvas becomes bothersome when you grapple with the fact that only native images can morph into other images. In short, text and imported images cannot disappear; you must cover them with something the same size or larger if you want to reuse that space. This can be overcome by giving each vignette, as represented by one row of storyboard content, a fresh space on the canvas and setting new camera positions accordingly. Other notable drawbacks about VideoScribe are its long processing time for exporting your final product relative to its length and the fact that some segments of the image library (e.g., drawings of public service personnel) are not relevant for American audiences. Since Sparkol is a UK company, it should be no surprise that their images, while inclusive, are Eurocentric.

Adobe Captivate

If we could have only one video creation program, it would be Adobe Captivate. It can be simple if you just want to record a PowerPoint presentation, synchronize it with audio, and add a couple of highlight boxes or pointer arrows. It can also handle complicated projects if you want to start from a blank project and arrange images, text, and video excerpts as you see fit. One laborsaving tip we have learned is to create a standard object style based on your institutional colors and fonts. The Object Style Manager provides options for importing and exporting Captivate styles files (.cps), so you can make a master style that can be applied to any later Captivate project. When picking object colors, consider them in relation to the screen content you will show the most. We began using purple arrows but, since the dominant color of our LibGuides is purple, we have transitioned to using blue for arrows and text box backgrounds. Even with careful planning, there will probably be content that requires a shift from your standard template. When we recorded a video in a database with a predominantly blue design scheme, our new blue objects had to undergo a color change once again to increase their distinctiveness within that environment.

For some institutions, the software we discussed may be out of reach due to financial or staffing constraints. For others, it may be too rudimentary or limited. If you have amazing artistic talent and a video camera, you can create tutorials like those published four to five years ago by Kimbel Library.[11] If you are looking for a free alternative to one of the technologies we discuss, you can try searching alternativeTo.[12] However, it should be no surprise that many of the comparisons are pale; for some paid technologies, there simply is no comparable alternative. Of the eleven alternatives for VideoScribe listed on alternativeTo, the clear leader by popular vote is Prezi. While you can accomplish similar things with both services, they are nowhere alike in terms of VideoScribe's engaging, artistic delivery. Some somewhat comparable options you may want to explore include GoAnimate, PowToon, Xtranormal, Moovly, and Wideo.

Step 4: Hosting and Distributing Your Videos

You will need a dependable virtual storage location that allows visitors to access videos easily and watch them without unnecessary interruptions such as buffering. In contrast with other, smaller files such as documents, video hosting requires a considerable amount of storage space plus available bandwidth. Internet connection speeds and bandwidth are generally not a problem for libraries and higher education institutions. However, if you want to serve the greatest number of visitors and make your videos accessible to those with slower Internet connections, you should choose a hosting solution that allows viewers with slower connections to lower the playback quality. YouTube provides a menu with multiple definition options and Vimeo provides an HD button that allows viewers to toggle into and out of high definition video.

The hosting solution you choose for your videos will depend on the technology already offered, supported, and/or allowed by your institution. Although Clemson University provides an in-house video hosting option, we chose to use YouTube for two main reasons. First, we wanted our videos to be familiar and findable. The ubiquity of the Google search and the integration of Google and YouTube mean that most if not all of our patrons have used YouTube at least once. At the very least, they should be somewhat familiar with its identity as a source for video content. For more Internet-savvy students, YouTube is likely the first place they look for instruction on topics from software tips and home improvement how-tos to video game cheats and walkthroughs. In short, YouTube is as close to the students' information searches as we can get our video content. As a provider of free hosting to just about anyone with an Internet connection, YouTube supports an incredibly diverse landscape, for better or worse. In evaluating potential hosting solutions, Vimeo was the other main contender as it is the other big name in free video hosting service and has much of the findability and familiarity of YouTube. Perhaps due only to our prior inexperience with Vimeo, we considered it to host content that was overall slightly more reputable. We had also heard a rumor from colleagues that YouTube claimed the rights to content posted to it. A careful reading of their terms of service led us to conclude that this was false, likely inspired by YouTube's need as a content distributor to reserve the right to use and display your content. The second reason we chose YouTube over Vimeo or an in-house option was the service's excellent closed captioning features. As we touched on in chapter 4, captioning should not be seen as an optional or bonus feature. Beyond being simply compelled by legal mandates or making accommodations after the fact, libraries should be proud to plan and provide content that is accessible. While YouTube can create automatic captioning for some videos, the turnaround time and accuracy can vary widely. After uploading short (one- or two-minute) videos, we have had some with automatic captions available minutes later and others that still did not have them the next day. When available, automatic captions are an excellent time saver, especially if you do not already have a video script or transcript. If YouTube "understands" your voice as well as ours, automatic captions can also be a source of levity in an otherwise tedious process. Among our favorites from our own videos are "deanna lee hamburger" (the MLA handbook), "high death" (high def.), and "I'm angry" (I'm Anne Grant). Of course, these examples illustrate why under no circumstances should you be content with leaving your automatic captions unedited.

We make recordings of synchronous workshops available only to those who attended them, so we leave those files in their original location on a server hosted by our IT department. We use YouTube to host all other videos. How you manage your YouTube account (called a channel) will depend on the audience you are trying to reach with your tutorials. YouTube at large is a place where content creators vie for search rankings and millions can be made in a single year.[13] We mention this not to make you contemplate a career change but to remind you that tutorial videos for higher education are not typical YouTube fare and should not be treated as such. One of the criteria for preferential search rankings is whether a video leads visitors to watch additional YouTube content. The primary purpose of our channel is to speak to (and occasionally about) the Clemson University community. Our tutorials are meant to inform viewers, not lure them into a procrastination vortex of funny animal videos, so we emphasize audience retention over other metrics such as search ranking or total video views. Of course, we would love if every Clemson student watched our videos; however, what we really want is that those who do (either willingly or through professor coercion) receive the best and most engaging content we can deliver.

A Snapshot of Our Efforts

Created on May 2, 2013, our YouTube channel currently hosts approximately forty videos, some of which are unpublished or private. For the lifetime of our channel (up until this chapter was written), our content had received 30,017 views with an average 83 percent viewed. Sixty-nine percent of total watch time has been via an embedded player, which is no surprise considering we embed videos in the library portion of our institution's required new-student class and within some of our LibGuides. What were surprises to us is that 23 percent of traffic was from suggested videos and that our videos have been shared forty-nine times. What these snapshot statistics do not make clear is this is data on all sixty-five videos that are or have ever been hosted on our channel. This includes first drafts of videos that received external review before being replaced with revised versions and videos created for internal training purposes. We suspect that our own captioning and quality control reviews have also inched upward our statistics for total views and audience retention. Since the data is collected, curated, and owned by YouTube, these statistics must be reviewed with a critical eye. For a free service, however, YouTube offers an amazing depth and quality of statistics. Despite the uncertainties and known error sources, our statistics show a tutorial program with strong overall quality and good return on investment. Considering the investment it can require to create dedicated tutorial videos, it is reasonable to be concerned that they will not be used. A recent global study showed that viewers now watch as much online video content as television.[14] Therefore, if you find your video content is not being viewed, consider making changes to its presentation structure, production quality, placement, or promotion.

Private, Public, and Unlisted Status of Videos

When we first upload a video, we have its default status set to private so that only we can see it while logged into our YouTube account. A public video is exactly what you would expect it to be; it will show on your channel and may appear as a search result or in suggested videos once someone has watched what YouTube's proprietary algorithm considers a "related" video. Unless a video is created with a specific, limited audience in mind, we make it public. While our tutorials likely have institution-specific references or resources, some of them may even be helpful for people outside our institution. We maintain videos created for a specific class, assignment, or other restricted audience as unlisted. They do not appear on our channel or in search results or suggestions but can be publicized via link distribution or embedding. When we create a video that needs review by someone outside the library such as a collaborating professor, we upload it as unlisted. We send the faculty member the link for access along with a solicitation for feedback and a caveat that it is not yet ready for distribution to students since it lacks captions and metadata.

Metadata for Videos

Your video title should describe the video topic as succinctly as possible. The description field is where you can provide the intended audience and learning outcomes plus any information about alternate versions (e.g., audio described, mobile-based) and specific contact information for more information. We add six to eight keywords with a few from YouTube's controlled vocabulary such as our institution and then a few colloquial terms about the video's topic and style. While YouTube does generate three automatic thumbnail options, the best and most appealing image will almost always be one you create and upload yourself. We generally play the video locally, take a screenshot of something we think is interesting yet representative, and crop that image tightly to the required dimensions of 1280 x 720 pixels. If there is nothing particularly eye-catching when shrunk to thumbnail size, you might consider creating and using a sort of title card with the topic and some institutional branding or additional bit of graphic appeal. When we posted our first videos to YouTube, we allowed comments and likes. Since then, we have disabled both for all of our videos. Thankfully, it was not due to a traumatic first-hand experience but rather a cautious consideration based on the general state of anonymous Internet comments. Our contact information is available with little effort should someone need to contact us regarding a video.

Distribution of your Videos

In order to put our tutorials at the point of need and minimize our viewers' exposure to ads and unrelated videos, we often embed our videos with LibGuides, Blackboard, or other websites. YouTube offers multiple options for player sizes as well as a custom size option. After we publish a new public video, we create a widget asset for it within LibGuides to make it easy for our guide authors to integrate it. We indicate the dimensions at the end of the asset name since we generally create a larger and a smaller version. Of course, this requires being or coordinating with your LibGuide administrator and keeping that system updated anytime a tutorial is replaced or deleted. If you decide the main access point for your tutorial content will be the channel itself, you will want to give your visitors a reason to return or subscribe to your channel. You should plan to release new videos regularly, such as once a week (your Tuesday Tip!) or the same day each month. In either case, you should probably also coordinate with your library's communication manager about posting a new video notice to your social media accounts, blog, or newsletter.

For us, the main drawback with YouTube hosting is its lack of link permanence. Updated versions of videos cannot simply drop into place of previous versions, meaning we must identify and update all locations where it is linked to or embedded. Since we are or work closely with the people that distribute video information, we have not kept a formal list of video access locations; however, it is an idea we are likely to implement as we expand marketing efforts for our tutorials. If you have the ability to create webpages (either within your library website or through a platform such as LibGuides), there is a potential solution for the link permanence conundrum. You can create a new page (and thus URL) for each video and embed the video player within it. That way the URL will still lead to the most recent version. This could be particularly useful should you provide a link to an instructor, since it is likely to make its way to and reside for years in a syllabus or course shell. If the video were eventually retired in favor of another type of content, you could have the page automatically redirect there. If you choose to use this solution for version control on YouTube, it would probably be best to apply it to all videos unless you are positive they cover content you will not need to address in any form after three or six months.

Step 5: Final Considerations for Planning and Organization

All video creation options require you to host and manage the video files, bringing about a series of questions to consider before you embark upon this endeavor. Some of these will be very familiar from the previous chapter, while others are unique to this type of learning object. Creating one tutorial means creating at least three files: your script, outline, or storyboard; the project file from your audiovisual creation software; and the video itself. However, this is the bare minimum that you will create and probably want to store for some duration. For example, using Audacity will create project files plus your final recording (e.g., mp3, WAV). Once we publish a video, we delete the Audacity project files and keep only the mp3. Trust us when we say that you need to get a file organization structure in place at least before you make more than one tutorial. We first began organizing tutorial files by type (e.g., scripts in one folder, supporting images in another) and it seemed like a good idea. Unfortunately, we realized after updating a couple of tutorials that this led to extraneous clicking and searching, which added up quickly. While it seems obvious in retrospect, using a folder per project is the method we should have chosen and what we have now begun to do. The only separation by file type we have continued is having all video files (e.g., mp4, WAV) together when you first open the folder. After our file reorganization, the "Supporting Files" folder now houses a folder with each tutorial title that houses everything used in the project to *create* the video. If you use a lot of supporting files per project and prefer not to have them intermingle (despite the "sort by file type" option), you may at this level want to put them in folders.

- How will you publicize and promote these videos? Embedding in your website? Institutional repository?
- Where will videos be hosted (for viewing by those outside the library)? Are there any limitations on individual file size, video length, total storage capacity, and so forth?
- Can you track accesses or views? If so, will you? How will you use this data?

- Who is in charge of managing videos on the hosting service and deactivating, archiving, or deleting recordings?
- How often will video content be reviewed for currency and accuracy? Will videos have an automatic "expiration date"? What types of things would make a video need to be replaced or unpublished before that date?
- Will videos be archived? If so, consider the same potential limitations as those for the hosting service.

To help us track our current and previously published videos, we developed a Microsoft Excel document. Speaking from experience, we highly recommend creating a document like this along with your first video and not retroactively once your Video Manager is well stocked. Our video master list has two sheets: one for videos currently on our channel and one for videos previously on our channel. The first sheet has columns for the video title, YouTube publication status, purpose, main content, version, expiration date, playlist(s), and subject matter contact. Our most recent addition to this spreadsheet was the playlists column. Deleting a video does not remove it from the playlist(s) to which it is assigned; instead, it just puts in its place the gray screen with ellipsis displayed for broken video links. Unfortunately, we discovered this only upon visiting one of our own playlists. The second sheet has columns for the video title, version, total views, publication date, removal date, and contact. When we add a new, first-version video to YouTube, we add its information to a new row on the first sheet. Just before we delete a video from our channel, we remove it from its playlist(s), cut and paste its spreadsheet row (with a couple of modifications) from the first sheet to the second, and record its total views and date of deletion.

There are many decisions involved as you begin to create online tutorials for your library instruction program. After taking into consideration how these videos will fit into your larger programming and branding and ensuring copyright and accessibility compliance, you will then need to make sure you choose the type of video that works with the technological capabilities of your instruction team. By taking this process one step at a time and making sure you do not lose sight of the bigger picture, creating instructional videos for your library can be a task that is well within your reach.

NOTES

1. "About the Licenses," *Creative Commons*, accessed November 3, 2015, http://creativecommons.org/licenses/.
2. "Section508.gov," *U.S. General Services Administration*, accessed November 3, 2015, http://www.section508.gov/.
3. "Presentation Software," *Prezi*, accessed November 24, 2015, https://prezi.com/.

4. "Animoto—Video Maker & Slideshow Player," *Animoto*, accessed November 24, 2015, https://animoto.com/.

5. "Test Your Mobile Sites and Responsive Web Designs," *MobileTest.me*, accessed November 3, 2015, http://mobiletest.me/.

6. Shunmuga S. Krishnan and Ramesh K. Sitaraman, "Video Stream Quality Impacts Viewer Behavior."

7. Ben Ruedlinger, "Does Length Matter?" *Wistia (blog)*, May 7, 2012, http://wistia.com/blog/does-length-matter-it-does-for-video-2k12-edition.

8. "Audacity," accessed November 3, 2015, http://audacityteam.org/.

9. "Audacity Manual," (October 26, 2015), http://manual.audacityteam.org/o/.

10. "Inkscape," accessed November 3, 2015, http://www.inkscape.org.

11. "Kimbel Library's Videos," *Vimeo*, accessed November 3, 2015, https://vimeo.com/kimbellibrary/videos.

12. "alternativeTo," accessed November 3, 2015, http://www.alternativeto.net/.

13. Grundberg and Hansegard, "YouTube's Biggest Draw Plays Games, Earns $4 Million a Year," *The Wall Street Journal*, June 16, 2014, http://on.wsj.com/1Rsk9b5.

14. Johnson, "From Teens to Adults, Everyone's Now Watching Online Video as Much as TV," *Adweek.(blog)*, October 14, 2015, http://www.adweek.com/news/technology/young-or-old-everyone-seems-online-video-much-tv-now-167541.

SIX
Bringing Library Staff On Board

One of the most challenging aspects of moving traditional library instruction online that you might face could be convincing your colleagues to give it a try. Teaching in the online environment is a huge transition and it can take people out of their comfort zones. It falls to the instruction leaders to make this transition as comfortable and open as possible. That will be easy, right? Well, here are some tips that might be helpful, but it would be misleading to think that there would not be bumps along the way. Creating buy-in from traditional library instructors to the online environment can be achieved by encouraging open and safe communication, providing lots of opportunity to practice, and by showing the benefits that can be gained from this new format.

STARTING THE CONVERSATION

Leading a group of diverse people anywhere, whether it is through the jungles of the Amazon or getting a bunch of librarians to try a new kind of teaching, requires constant communication, and while you may not be shouting for people to "watch out for that snake" (as you might in the Amazon) you will need to be ready to do the equivalent when confronting the perils of online teaching. The first step in your communication plan might be to make sure people understand the importance of teaching online in a just-in-time environment, but instead of telling them what to think, use a session where you ask pointed questions and allow them to draw their own conclusions. Before we start talking about the kinds of questions you can ask at such a session, it is important to talk about ways to set the stage for such a conversation. You will want to make sure that people know the questions ahead of time and that you are asking these questions to *start* a conversation and not to make any definite decisions in that particular meeting. You might want to emphasize that it is an idea-sharing meeting and that each person should feel free to bring their excitement or their reservations and that they will be able to discuss them openly. You may even want to ask that people contribute to a set of ground rules for the meeting. Examples might include

- Do not interrupt others when they are speaking
- Be respectful
- Come prepared to contribute
- Speak only for yourself
- Create a safe environment for new ideas

While many of these concepts might seem to be common sense, when you start discussions that could potentially change the fundamental ways that a person does their job (moving traditionally taught face-to-face workshops online) conversations can get heated before people are even aware of what is happening.

Once you have set your ground rules, here are some ideas for questions to get these conversations started:

- What does successful library instruction look like (subject classes, tours, reference interactions, etc.)?
- What are the most effective forms of instruction?
- What unique things do you want our instruction to do?
- Who is our *real* target audience for instruction (who cares the most)?
- How do we best reach our target audience?
- Institutionally, how do we get our instruction out there?
- Where do you see instruction growing or shrinking?
- What strategies do you use in the classroom (face-to-face or online) to teach about library resources?
- How do you think drop-in library workshops have been going? What would you change? What would you leave the same?
- Would you teach a workshop online? Why or why not?
- Do you see yourself using tutorials in your teaching? If so, how? If not, why not?
- If you were going to create five short "library tips" tutorials, what would they address?
- What kind of support do you need with regard to instruction?

After you get people talking openly about some of their fears and concerns, or even about what they are looking forward to or wanting to explore, you can start to address these hurdles directly and help people with a possible transition. Now, we are not promising that you will hear what you want to hear as a result of asking these kinds of questions. In fact, you may find at the end of this conversation that face-to-face instruction makes more sense for your campus populations, but if that is the case, no worries! You can continue to hone and improve those workshops by perhaps changing the length and creating fifteen-minute "turbo sessions" instead of fifty-minute workshops. Alternatively, you could work toward creating conference-like full-day workshops that target certain needs and populations. One such event might be a graduate student boot camp that brings your campus writing center, library, career center, and technology folks to one place and allows time for grad students to write while having support directly on hand. You also may find that you just have a couple of instructors who are interested in moving online and that is okay, too. That means you have a base of people who will be invested in being successful in teaching online and that makes the process much easier for you!

BLENDED LIBRARIANSHIP

Another way to get the conversation going about teaching online is to discuss the concept of the blended librarian. This concept began with an article by Steven Bell and John Shank in *College and Research Library News* in 2004 and has sparked a continuously developing conversation because it changes a great deal about the traditional roles of librarians.[1]

> Blended librarianship is intentionally not library centric (i.e., focused on the building and its physical collections) but, rather, it is librarian centric (i.e., focused on people's skill, knowledge they have to offer, and relationships they build). It focuses on answering why librarians matter to provide compelling reasons for why academic libraries remain essential and indispensable to the academy. In the future, the library as place and the containers its collections come in should not define the librarian as it has too often done in the past. Instead, the services (e.g., course related instruction) and products (i.e., information) provided by the librarians should.[2]

Since the concept of blended librarianship brings together instructional design and technology, it is a good fit for conversations about expanding library instruction in the online environment. Sometimes if you can encourage "outside of the box" thinking in a broad sense, before you start talking about logistics, you can get better buy-in from more traditional instructors.

By focusing your conversation on the skills that your teaching librarians bring to your institution, you can begin to talk about better ways to bring that information to those who are using the library resources. This concept allows librarians to think about new tools for teaching and new opportunities for topics of discussion because as the role of the library expands beyond the physical collection to unique services provided, librarians can use online workshops and tutorials to describe new services like data management consulting, citation management tools, and data visualization.

TOURING THE ONLINE CLASSROOM

Now that you have people talking and you have a core group of library instructors who want to learn more, you need to start setting up times to practice and observe. At this stage in the process, you should already have chosen a teaching platform. Based on our own expertise and experience, we will pretend that we have selected Adobe Connect for our online classroom technology. First, you should decide whether to create and host a single classroom or allow multiple "rooms." Since each room will have its own URL, it is important to decide on this first so you can communicate it to your instructors. When planning instruction for your instructors, you may also wish to create a "sandbox" room into which they can be turned loose to play without fear of deleting, modifying, or interrupting something important. Next, you will want to get your group into the classroom and let them look around. For some, it may be the first time they have ever been in that space. Others may have visited often but, in either case, you need to have some sort of basic structure for this first venture into the official online library classroom space.

First, set up a time to "meet" in the classroom by sending an email with a link and provide simple instructions for logging in along with information that they might need for installing microphones, video cameras, or software. As the group arrives, greet them as if they were coming into a physical classroom. Not only does this help to make them feel comfortable, it also models how instructors can work to make the online environment friendly and welcoming to students and faculty who will eventually be attending the sessions. Once everyone is in the classroom, be prepared to offer a very brief sample workshop that includes slides and perhaps one interactive activity. To kill two birds with one stone, you can use this mini presentation to teach them how to teach in the online space by using the following outline:

- Introduce yourself with a picture or video.
- Tell them about the use of chat and how they can create private chats with you or another classmate (you can send someone a message directly as you talk).
- Show them how to use any features you want to highlight, such as polls, the whiteboard, or screen sharing.

Once your group has been acclimated, elevate their classroom status to instructor so they can see the administrative side of the environment. In the screenshot of our online classroom, there is a presenter-only area to the right that we often refer to metaphorically as "behind the curtain."

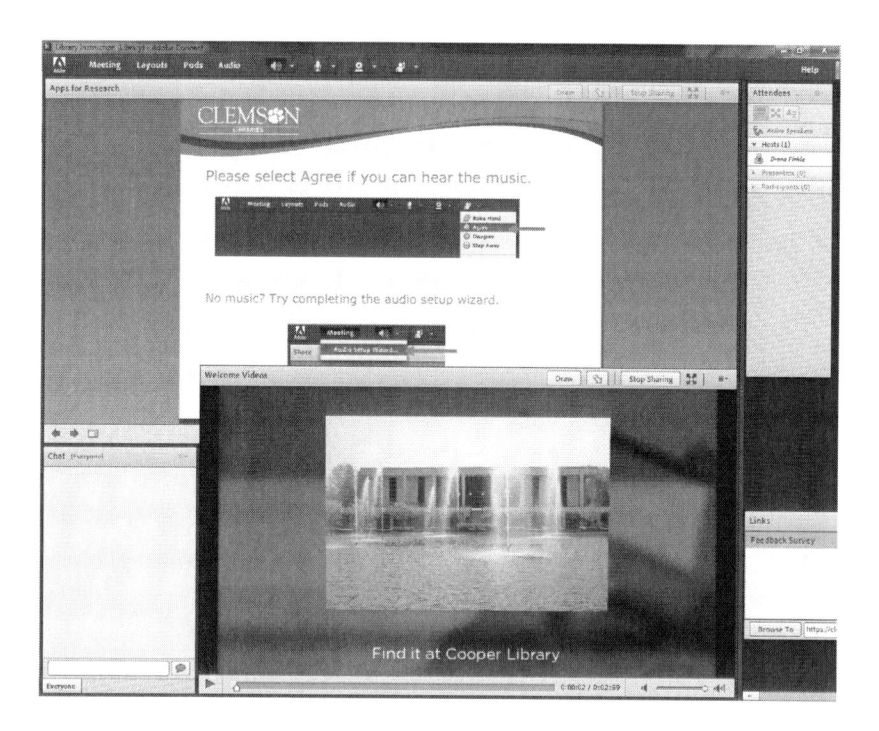

Figure 6.1. Online Classroom with Presenter-Only Area

You will notice the attendee pod there as well as the link for our session feedback survey so we remember to deploy it at the end of each session (hopefully). Allow time for your classroom visitors to look around and get the feel of their abilities in this mode, letting them know that you are there if they have any questions. After the session is over, follow up with the participants and ask them

- What did you like most?
- What did you like least?
- What concerns you most about teaching in this environment?
- What is one idea that you have for using the tools in the online classroom in your sessions?

You can use the responses to these questions to create later training and practice opportunities as well as to plan sample sessions for them to observe. By creating an environment for practice, you will be continuing to offer ways for the library instructors to communicate openly and when they know that you will respond to their questions, they will probably continue to work toward teaching online.

PRACTICE, PRACTICE, PRACTICE

Now that your instructors are familiar with the online classroom, encourage them to get started! You might want to plan to host a series of mini sessions that last anywhere from five to fifteen minutes on topics such as

- Finding eBooks
- Locating a journal article
- Booking a study room
- Using a citation generator or bibliography manager

You can attend these sessions alongside the instructors to provide technical and emotional support, responding to any questions in the chat and assisting any of the participants who are having difficulty hearing or seeing the content. If you choose to record the session, it can provide the instructor with an opportunity to review their performance and you might even consider providing them with a self-evaluation form that might include such questions as

- Did you speak in a clear, measured tone?
- Were you able to respond to questions from participants?
- Did you feel as though participants were engaged in the session?
- Was the content clearly communicated?
- What do you think went really well during this session?
- How might you improve?

If you feel particularly daring, you can invite instructors to observe an online session that you teach and ask that they provide any backup you might need and then allow them to complete an evaluation of your session using the same questions. This allows them to explore the online space a bit more safely and can also provide opportunities for your own growth in online spaces. Another option for increasing awareness and experience in online learning is to offer sessions to other library employees as internal training opportunities as there will be some instructors who may feel more comfortable presenting to peers than to library patrons.

CREATING ONLINE ACTIVITIES

It is important to remember that part of the conversation about moving sessions online is the recognition that teaching in the online environment is inherently different from teaching face to face and instructors must plan accordingly. You will need to make sure that your instructors know that they will not simply be able to teach the classes they have always taught and that they will need to become familiar with both the tools in the online classroom and the differences in the level of interaction they will have with their attendees. In the online classroom, there is less room for the "sage on the stage" kind of teaching and a greater need to involve learners in the session. If they already incorporate interactivity for face-to-face sessions, some of this interaction may translate almost seamlessly. There is little difference between demonstrating truncation in ink on a dry erase board and online with a whiteboard feature. The chat box can take the place of asking students to call out ideas or suggestions verbally and is likely a more comfortable interaction for many students. Table 6.1 shows some other ideas for moving traditional instruction online.

You might also ask your instructors to go out and find examples of recorded online sessions on any number of topics to gather ideas for activities that would work best in their own sessions. There are many massive open online courses (MOOCs) that can provide both good and bad examples of online learning, but what your instructors will notice (and probably have already noticed) about teaching online is that it is not okay to simply lecture for an extended period of time online. They will want to keep their sessions active and engaging or they will risk having

Table 6.1.

Traditional Activity	Online Activity
Present students with a research question and ask them to tell you which words they would choose as keywords.	Activate the whiteboard feature, type the research question, and then ask students to write on the board or draw lines under/to what they think would be the best keywords.
Demonstrate how to use a database and then let students do some individual searches while you walk around observing and answering questions.	Briefly demonstrate a search in a database and then ask/allow a student to share their screen and demonstrate their own search. Ask for peer feedback in the chat.
Ask students an informal question such as, "How many of you have been to the library in the past week?"	Create an interactive poll with the question and response options so students can answer anonymously.
Break students into small groups to share a computer and work on an activity.	Create "break out" rooms, assign students to groups to meet online about an activity, and then have them present to the class. If your software does not allow for this, you could use Google Hangouts.
Ask students to suggest a topic.	Ask students to suggest a topic via chat or the whiteboard.
Hand out a print copy of a sample article so students can examine it and determine whether it is scholarly.	Share the document on your screen and allow students to either download or look at it in on the screen to determine its quality.

their attendees wander off to check their Facebook page in the middle of their library lesson. Once you know of a few librarians who have experienced some online session, it might be a good opportunity to have a group discussion to talk about the good, the bad, and the ugly parts of their experiences and how it could have been improved. You could even include a brief assessment piece that your librarians could complete after they participate in an online professional development opportunity to get them thinking about their own online instruction. For example, you could ask,

- What did you find helpful in the session you just attended?
- What did you find distracting?
- Was the session interactive in any way? If so, how?
- Did you find that your attention wandered from the presentation? How might the presenter have done a better job keeping your focus on their topic?

You could ask for the responses to these information surveys and then compile them to encourage a discussion about library instruction in your own department.

COPYRIGHT CONSIDERATIONS

As mentioned in chapter 5, when teaching online, there are some things to consider about copyright that might vary from the face-to-face classroom environment. As long as your institution has a copyright policy, you are probably covered by the Technology, Education, and Copyright Harmonization (TEACH) Act. Enacted in 2002, the TEACH Act allows both distance and face-to-face educational environments to transmit or display copyrighted work to students enrolled in the course in which the material is being used. You will want to make sure that any images that you use in presentations have the proper citations, just as you would in a face-to-face session. If you share a video, it is best to share a link and not embed or share the video itself in the online classroom. Not only will you want to make sure that students can hear it (you will probably have to send a link instead of showing the video in your browser), you will also want to make sure you have considered whether its inclusion would be covered under fair use. If you use YouTube, you will want to do your best to make sure that the content you are sharing is legally provided as there are many instances on YouTube when content has been accessed and reproduced illegally. You will also want to make sure if you distribute a copy of an article that you send a link, including the proxy, to ensure that students are accessing the information legally provided to them within the terms of existing database contracts. Another copyright consideration might be thinking about utilizing cleared music as the session gets started so that attendees can check their volume and ability to hear what is going on in the classroom. At Clemson, we chose to upload some video files of music-based "library commercials" we created using Animoto, the web-based slideshow tool we talked about in chapter 5.

Creating buy-in both internally and externally for online library workshops takes consistent and open communication, lots of practice with online teaching tools and techniques, and the ability to help librarians and university administrators understand the role of the library in the online environment. There can be a tendency on campus for the library to continue to be seen as a "book box" used for storage of information rather than a dynamic, multifaceted information management resource. Furthermore, those working and studying at a distance may feel disconnected from library services because they do not have easy access to the physical buildings and take for granted that the library invests its time and money in enabling such seamless remote access. Creating effective online learning tools can help bridge the gap and provide ubiquitous access to the wealth of knowledge that library instructors have to offer.

NOTES

1. Steven Bell and John Shank, "The Blended Librarian," *College & Research Library News* 65, no. 7 (2004): 372–75.

2. John Shank, Steven Bell, and Diane Zabel, "Blended Librarianship," *Reference & User Services Quarterly* 51, no. 2 (2011): 106.

SEVEN
Marketing Online Workshops

The movement of library instruction to the online environment is only one way that librarians are seeking to meet the just-in-time needs of their patrons. Marketing of this type of instruction should reflect these changes by speaking directly to the needs of the patrons rather than to the topic of the sessions. This sounds ridiculous, but will be explained in just a bit. Effective marketing of online workshops is best achieved by making a plan, diversifying modes of outreach, and by creating consistency with the library and university brands and goals.

The decision to move workshops online should be one that is made with purpose and a vision for the big picture. It is important for you to determine the larger goal for the library instruction plan and how these new online workshops will fit into that goal and then to determine how these goals for library instruction fit into the larger university goals. When you do this, it will help with buy-in from university administration and can provide strength for the outreach and marketing campaigns. At Clemson, we plan our instruction events for the academic year during the summer so that we can have a calendar on which to build our marketing plan. If you decide to do the same, here are some questions to ask as you plan your session schedule:

- How many online sessions will be offered during the semester?
- How long should a standard session be? Will you offer any "mini" sessions?
- At what point in the semester would the content be most relevant to students?
- What days and times would be best for your target audience? Does your institution publish standard class meeting times for each semester (to help avoid scheduling conflicts)?

- Is it important that students sign up in advance or can they just "show up"?
- How are you going to communicate the room URL and other room access basics?

The interesting thing about marketing is that it, in and of itself, can almost be considered a form of instruction because if you can create an awareness of the kinds of workshops and opportunities that the library will provide, even if a person does not attend the event, they know more about the library than they did before. This being said, the marketing plan should be considered before the first workshop outline is even created. In the academic library environment, this starts with a careful examination of the academic calendar and even with selected faculty syllabi. Ask yourself these questions:

- When are projects due?
- What kinds of research will be required?
- When will students likely begin working on assignments?
- How can the library meet needs of students working on these projects?
- Are there areas where collaboration with other campus support organizations would make sense?

The marketing of your workshops will prove to be almost as important as the content, so as you begin to formulate your marketing plan you will want to consider four main areas: audience, marketing format, placement and timing, and assessment.

AUDIENCE

Considering your audience is absolutely crucial for both planning content and marketing your workshops. After answering some of the questions previously mentioned, you should begin to have an idea of the kinds of workshops you are planning to provide and you should have a good idea of the audience as well. If they are workshops that are not geared towards a particular class or assignment (because those should be pretty easy to market to individual professors and classes), you need to think about who would be interested in the topics and who would be attracted to the flexibility of the online environment. If your institution has a dedicated office to coordinate online programming, contact them with information about your workshops well in advance so that they can distribute the information to their network of online instructors. You might also scan your course catalog for courses that are being taught online and perhaps even follow up by looking into online syllabus repositories to make sure your workshops fit in with existing assignments. You might also want to visit any off-campus locations (if possible) and if you are a part of a land grant institution, you may want to visit any extension or research sites to gauge the needs of those audiences. If you are not able to visit physically, you may want to send out a survey. We provide an example of one such survey in the appendix. Another consideration for your audience will be generational. Older students may prefer later hours as they work around full-time job schedules. They may also be coming back to school after an extended absence and want more in-depth training that includes some basic technology training. Younger students may want less detail and more pointed tips, possibly also in an evening session but in a shorter format or something scheduled between standard class times so they can squeeze it in during the day. For example, we offered an online session in the evening called "Return to Research" targeting our nontraditional students and it was quite well attended. Yet no matter who your audience is, they will want to know from your marketing why they should spend precious time attending your workshop, so you need to spend some time crafting a marketing plan that lets them know what is in it for them.

BRANDING AND GOALS

As you plan both marketing and online workshops, do not forget that your communication does not take place in a vacuum. You are going to want to make sure that you comply with any visual identity standards that have already been established by your library and your institution as a whole. For instance, if you use PowerPoint slides in your online workshops, you should use colors from the university palette and preferred fonts. These same colors and fonts should also be used on any digital signage, images posted on social media or on monitors across campus, and print handouts or tear-aways. If your library has a communication coordinator or public relations representative, this person should be your first contact. If not, you should search your institution's website for information. Terminology can vary by institution, but common things to look for are a brand toolkit, media resources, style guide, identity standards, or communication guidelines. Universities and other organizations have brand standards for a reason. They give people guidelines to be creative while still "sounding like" the institution. You get to use its credibility and the respect it garners in your audience's attention span. While you may have to sacrifice a bit of your personal creativity, you can trust that people whose job it is to do such things made decisions about required colors, fonts, and other guidelines after considerable thought and possibly even research. Cooperating with your institution's guidelines will help enforce the library's role as integral to the institution and create a familiar appearance for your items, which lets people "tune in" to them.

Your institution may have expectations and specifications about any or all of the following:

Logo or Word Mark

The good news is someone should be able to provide you with a good-quality image. They may even provide variations such as a one-color version or versions best suited for dark backgrounds. The less good news is there are likely stipulations on the size, orientation, placement, background color, or usage of the image.

Color Palette

You can probably find your institution's color palette with specifications for various media (e.g., HTML, RGB, CMYK) and perhaps even downloadable swatches for common desktop publishing programs such as Microsoft Office Suite and Adobe InDesign. Some institutions have only two or three official colors, often at high contrast to each other, which can pose a challenge for creating appealing designs. You may need to work with shades of those colors to make something that hits the right place on the spectrum between boring and (figuratively) making viewers' eyes bleed. If your institution has a secondary palette—one that includes colors beyond your traditional "school colors"—take a moment right now to acknowledge your good fortune. Since Clemson University has ten secondary colors (even after one overlooks the fact that they renamed true black), it is easy to find an acceptable color that works for a particular event. As with all professionally chosen color palettes, all of the options look at least decent when paired. However, added variety makes it especially important that we consider color contrast and keep text accessible. Our go-to tool for checking color contrast is WebAIM's Color Contrast Checker.[1] We ensure the text and background of anything published digitally has enough contrast to comply with Web Content Accessibility Guidelines (WCAG) AA standards. With a set color palette, it only takes a few minutes to run all your likely permutations and establish once and for all whether that brown background can be used with tan text. If any of this information is new to you, the parent site of the tool we use has a wealth of information on web accessibility.

Font

Again, this is institution-specific whether there are any requirements or even recommendations. If there are requirements, your institution will likely provide several options and even suggestions on when to use them. These fonts will likely be ones that are already included in basic desktop publishing programs or will be provided upon request. If you have some leeway (or no official recommendations) regarding fonts, it is still a good idea to choose one or two fonts that you will use for most of your communication. You should choose one font without serifs (e.g., Arial) since this style is usually used in electronic communication, appears uncluttered, and conveys a modern feel. You should also choose a font with serifs (e.g., Georgia) to use when you want contrast for headings or to put forth something that feels more traditional or formal. Even if you enjoy installing fonts on your computer, these fonts should be commonly available in Microsoft Office and other communication and desktop publishing programs. Trust us that publishing is hard enough using special fonts provided freely for installation from our university and you do not want to risk a wonky bookmark (or sending your co-worker detailed download and installation instructions) because you picked some beautiful font that is only available through this certain website. That said, there are definitely times when a special font is just what you need for a marketing item. There are multiple sites that offer free font downloads, but we like to search dafont.com for free-to-download options. Just remember, your unique font should be easy to read and should probably be used sparingly (such as for a punchy session title) rather than for all the text.

You also want to make sure that any online workshops that you plan fit into university and library goals. The exponential growth of online programs provides a prime opportunity for this platform of library instruction as it fits naturally into the digital environment. When these workshops are applied to the larger university goals of increasing the success of online students, they become a crucial piece of this growing area of higher education.

As you move some of your traditional face-to-face workshops online, you have a fantastic opportunity to highlight this new mode of instruction to your audience and the implementation of a well-structured marketing plan can serve both as an excellent way to attract attendees and as an extension of the instruction that you are providing. Online workshops have the ability to meet the patron no matter where they are located. Some will attend the workshops from the second floor of the library, while others may attend from across the ocean. Effective marketing of online workshops is best achieved by making a plan, diversifying modes of outreach, and by creating consistency with the library and university brands and goals.

MARKETING FORMATS

Faculty and students are overwhelmed by their email and yet, this is probably one of the most reliable and even most requested ways that they would like to be notified about learning opportunities on campus.

However, just like it is important to diversify with your money, it is also important not to put all of your marketing pieces in one place. You will want to consider placing ads in a variety of locations, which can mean in a variety of formats.

- Send an email to key faculty and students that briefly outlines relevant classes and speaks directly to needs they may have.
- Request time to speak at on-campus meetings such as student and faculty senates, orientations, and departmental meetings.
- Create print fliers for target audiences such as one that outlines top services for faculty or graduate students.
- Design digital signage for specific locations such as a piece in the campus gym that advertises opportunities to "Train Your Brain" with library workshops.
- Make use of whiteboards and even bathroom mirrors for "guerilla marketing" by highlighting workshops of interest.
- Create tear-away fliers to post in residence halls, student unions, and on departmental bulletin boards providing catchy phrases to speak to the needs of that particular audience.
- Write articles for library and university blogs.
- Create tweets and Facebook posts.

It can be difficult to wrap your head around the idea of having to "push" the library workshops to your audience because traditionally the library has not been an aggressor when it comes to sharing information about services; however, with new competition in the provision of information there come new roles in teaching about how to find the best possible resources.

PLACEMENT AND TIMING

The timing of marketing is crucial to the visibility of library instruction. In his book *Marketing Today's Academic Library,* Brian Mathews speaks of envisioning the semester in phases.[2] In the first phase, at the beginning of the academic year, you provide an introduction to the library since at this point many students are just beginning their semester and do not have any current projects. This phase might include posters, emails, digital signage, and tutorials that cover an overview of library services. It also may include pieces that assist faculty with posting eReserves or finding the library on your school's learning management system. While it can be difficult to plan out all library instruction before the academic year begins, it is a good idea to try to schedule as much as you can so that you can begin to get a bigger picture around which you can plan your marketing activities.

Figure 7.1. Cover of Instruction Menu Brochure

Here are some suggested steps for approaching the coordination of your workshops and your marketing plan:

1. Create a working calendar—You can do this electronically or in print. Electronic options include a Google Calendar or an Outlook Calendar dedicated to planning your workshop and marketing schedule. Print options include lots of available online calendar templates that are freely available.
2. Enter academic calendar information—Record any holidays, midterms, exams, or other momentous events that will impact your audiences. Once you can see when students will probably have a lot of projects due, you can begin to schedule workshops around needs that they may have in the moment. With the move to just-in-time instruction, you have to be ready with your instruction when they need it and not months ahead of time.

3. Enter any preplanned instruction activities—Now it is time to plug in your online workshops! Where will they be needed most? What kinds of topics will be relevant at what times? Perhaps offer a couple of introductory, lunchtime sessions at the beginning of the semester. Then, as midterms approach you could offer some evening sessions that serve as reminders for ways to find good resources quickly.
4. Enter marketing planning—Once you can see where your instruction is going to take place, you can start to build those waves of marketing and awareness. If you have a workshop planned for a Friday, plan to begin "talking" about it on social media that Monday. If it is a big event, you may want to put out one or two "save-the-date" or teaser posts. If you know that midterms are coming, plan a marketing campaign and bundle some of your workshops into a themed "package" of help sessions with their own marketing identifier such as "last minute librarian" or "procrastination destination." Plan to post digital signage a day or two before workshops take place and also structure any email contact in a timely manner as to maximize impact.

You may find that the needs students might have will change the types of workshops you provide. For example, if your institution has an organized research fair or exhibit that is scheduled for a certain time of year, often students will be required to present a poster that describes their research. Two or three weeks prior to this event would be an excellent opportunity for the library to provide a workshop series in collaboration with the technology group and perhaps the writing center that might fall under the leading question: "Do you need to create a research poster?" Then, the library could offer a workshop about using the best resources, the writing center could offer tips on ensuring that the wording is effective and citations are correct, and the technology group could provide information on designing and printing the posters. If these sessions were offered as a series of tutorials, students could access them whenever they are working on their posters, even if it is 3 a.m.!

Planning is key to marketing success. If you can get a big picture of what is coming up during the semester, you can begin to figure out what you will need to support and market all of the pieces of instruction that you will offer during the semester. You will also use this plan to create a budget for any giveaways or print fliers you may want to offer to increase awareness of your programming. You may want to include any prizes for contests or incentives for completing feedback forms that you might include in your plans. When we think of the timing for marketing library online workshops, we picture a wave. In the days leading up to the class, we build up interest via social media posts or fliers, then we hold the event (the crest of the wave, of course!), and finally we follow up with appreciation for attendance or even pictures of the session on our blog and social media. This kind of placement and timing keeps the library and its sessions on people's radar and can build up interest for the next event.

CLASSROOM CALENDARS

In addition to the marketing and event calendars, we also maintain a calendar for the classroom itself. If you have a small group of instructors, a shared Outlook or Google calendar or even a printed calendar posted in a central location may suit your needs. Depending on how many online sessions you have going on, there is probably little chance that one person is going to schedule and promote something that happens to be during another instructor's session. Depending on the online classroom technology you use, however, you may also need to track and prevent sessions from being scheduled during system downtime. Having an internal classroom calendar also means that instructors can easily communicate their need for coverage should they find themselves with a schedule conflict or sick day. While you can offer a semester of online sessions without maintaining an external calendar, providing one will allow eager students to plan ahead and avoid missing out on a topic that is offered multiple times.

When we first began offering online sessions, we used a homegrown solution for online registration. Visitors to the webpage had to log in with valid university credentials before being able to register for *or even see* the classes offered. In this age of long, complex passwords and smartphone visitors, we suspected this burden was a deterrent to our would-be students. We also quietly acknowledged the irony of out-the-gate exclusiveness when trying to offer free learning opportunities led by advocates of information sharing. From a practical standpoint, this registration system also had some other significant flaws. Events could be viewed only in a list presented in chronological order. There was no way to reorganize by session title, for example, and no method of getting a holistic calendar view (unless you felt like entering them all on your personal one). There was also no event tagging or filtering, leaving potential students to read each event description and more savvy ones to employ the page search for keywords such as "online" or "citation."

Two years ago, we were able to switch from this in-house registration solution to the LibCal product from Springshare. Our adoption of this service was primarily for its room booking capability, but we were more than pleased with the benefits LibCal's calendars offered over our previous registration system. Our institution currently subscribes to a paid tier with fifty available calendars since we use LibCal to manage our study and meeting room bookings; however, Springshare does offer a free version that supports three room schedules and three event calendars.[3] We created a public calendar for all instruction events. It is worth noting we have also used a private calendar for the working calendar created along with our marketing plan. When creating an event calendar in LibCal, you will need to input your location and campus options. We also chose to set up event categories and establish a color scheme based on our institutional palette. It is worth noting that all of the event color options provided in LibCal are WCAG AA compliant and most are WCAG AAA compliant. [4] However, we still found the event information a bit hard to read and also wanted to reinforce our institutional brand identity. Using our institutional palette as a base, we selected six distinct colors that were light enough to meet WCAG AAA standards for color contrast. In keeping with accessibility best practices, the color scheme does not provide new information; rather, it simply corresponds with the event category set in the system. While a custom color scheme is aesthetically pleasing, it may not be worth the effort as these new values cannot be displayed in place of the default color swatches; within LibCal version 1, this meant a notable amount of copy-pasting hexadecimal color codes either from existing events or from our in-house LibCal guide. Also within our LibCal guide we have a box for "Online Session Boilerplate" that reads, "This session is held in [our online classroom]—attend from anywhere! Headphones or speakers are required. Microphone is optional. Please log in five minutes before the session's start time and contact us if you have any technical difficulties, and includes the instructions to paste this text as the final paragraph of the session description. Since we use only one instance of an online classroom, there is only one URL; the text in square brackets is the descriptive title of that link.

Another benefit of using LibCal for event management is the ability to generate full-size or miniature calendar widgets (or event lists) that can be embedded within another webpage. Of course, LibCal integrates well with LibGuides (as long as you are using the same version for both). There are also about a dozen retrieval-only application program interfaces (more commonly known as APIs) available within the Admin menu. This means your LibCal data can be accessed by and integrated into another website if you have the opportunity and/or expertise to do so. The miniature instruction calendar displayed below has been customized both with LibCal's provided options and some custom CSS implemented by an amiable and accommodating library tech support worker.

Event Calendars

Using LibCal for your event scheduling and registration means you have one central place (albeit virtual) to which you can point students as you publicize your workshops. Of course, creating a new calendar means you have to get the word out about it. If your library already hosts one-

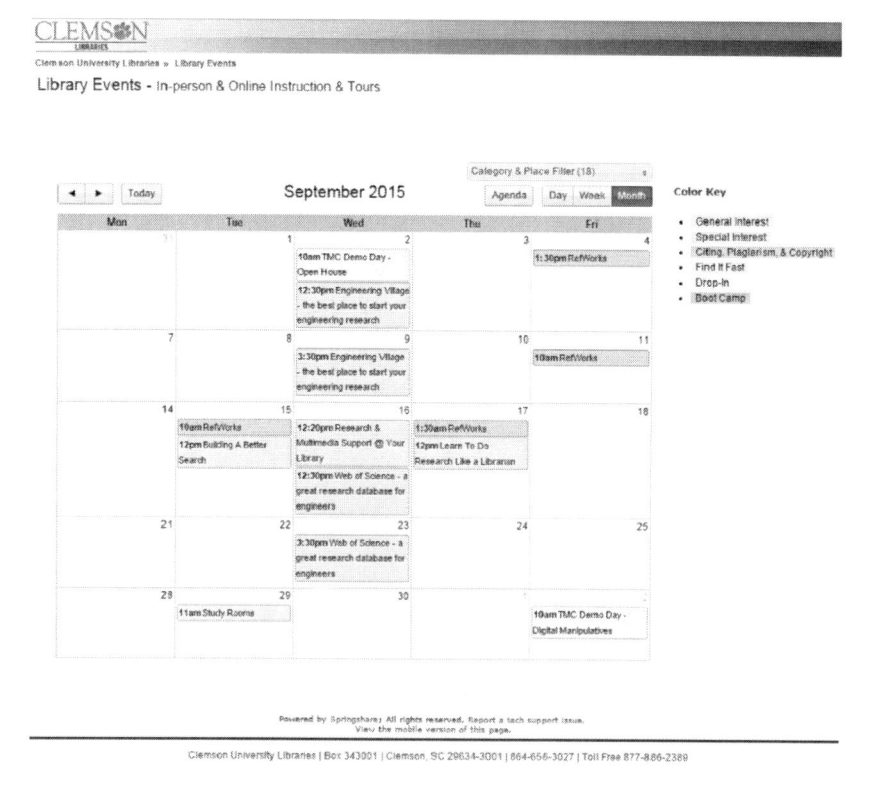

Figure 7.2. Public Events Calendar Homepage

time or recurring events (e.g., exam stress busters, Banned Books Week), it probably already has a calendar that it publishes regularly. If it is digital, this would mean some duplication of information and effort since LibCal already provides events in calendar view. However, this is likely worth the effort since the library-wide calendar should have an established audience, workflow, and perhaps even a publicity or distribution system. If there is a print version, you will need to think carefully about what information you can provide within the existing space and style restrictions.

The Institutional Events Calendar

Many colleges and universities publish and maintain an events calendar in addition to the formal, often fixed (i.e., PDF or printed) academic calendar. At Clemson, there is an electronic events calendar where instructional sessions and promotional events can be posted.[5] It is relatively simple to add events and events can be categorized and added to personal calendars from this system. For example, if the library knows

Instruction Calendar

Figure 7.3. Embedded Instruction Calendar

that it has a series of instructional sessions, we can fill out a spreadsheet with the title, description, time, and location and send it to the calendar administrator who will then upload and tag the events with the appropriate information. While this kind of platform can be useful, it can also be intimidating as it includes all other social, academic, and promotional events on campus.

It is useful to learn before you list your events what, if any, data you could access about views and registrations. Our institutional event calendar has a way for people to indicate whether they are going or went to an event, but there is no official registration system to verify whether they actually did attend. If using a calendar of this type, you would need to prompt interested students to take the additional step of completing your registration form (assuming you choose to require or encourage registration). For maximum accessibility and usability, this means your listing will include a descriptive link to either the event page within your system or the event registration form. Before you list your events, you will also need to find out how and when to communicate any cancellations or other special situations that occur. Above all, your presence within the institutional calendar should follow the Hippocratic Oath and "do no harm." If you are going to have a presence, make sure it is professional and leaves that audience with a favorable or at least neutral impression of your library and its instruction. In the end, you must evaluate the pros and cons of publicizing your events in this manner and decide whether it may be worth the time and effort.

Special Events Calendars

Campus organizations that serve specific demographics may maintain their own events calendar. For example, our program for new freshmen and transfer students hosts numerous events during the first weeks of fall semester. Since we are already involved in new student orientation through the course we mentioned in previous chapters, we were asked to submit any events we thought would be relevant to this population for inclusion in the events area of a new student smartphone app. While we did not receive any statistics from the app or notice an increase in workshop attendance, participation required little effort and we would definitely do it again next year. Regardless of whether you end up creating joint workshops with the campus stakeholders you identified (see chapter 3), you should consider asking them if there are ways they might be willing and able to publicize your events. Just having some fliers about your copyright and course reserves workshops at a new faculty orientation could help you reach out to professors who might otherwise have considered their library just for checking out books and buying journal subscriptions.

SESSION REGISTRATION

While requiring any type of registration may be a deterrent to your students, we do ask that our students sign up in advance for classes. Of course, we do not stand at the virtual door as gatekeepers and would not eject a student from the classroom upon discovering they had not registered. Using a session registration system has multiple benefits that, for our needs and community, outweigh the potential chilling effect. Our standard registration form asks only the student's name and email address. It does not require that the email address have the institutional suffix (i.e., @clemson.edu). This basic registration form provides us with just enough information so that we can contact students before a session if necessary. This has been useful on the rare occasions we have had to cancel a session since we were able to know there were students that had planned to attend (at least enough to register) and access a list of their email addresses to contact them about the schedule change. Having email addresses of attendees will also allow you to send out preparatory materials or links (should you host that type of session) as well as your slides (or a link to them in your institutional repository) after the fact. If you ever do email your attendees, we want to take a second and advocate for putting their addresses in the BCC field so their information is not distributed to others. Yes, with our classroom technology the students "see" each other in the room when they attend the session; however, it is just good practice to protect your students' privacy as much as possible. Depending on your registration system and the work you want to put into maintaining it, you may wish to ask for more information during registration. You could shift your data collection from during or after the session and into registration, although you would want to take care not to overburden registrants or cause negative sentiment that leads them to bail on the actual session. Reconciling your registration list against the attendees at your session will provide you an accurate attendance record. If you choose to reward attendees of multiple sessions with a library prize, draw an awardee from among those that attended a session, or allow professors to assign your sessions for (extra) credit, you will want attendance information beyond a simple number. Knowing the names of your attendees means that you may be able to look up their status (e.g., student, staff) and perhaps their year and major of study. Depending on the privacy guidelines of your library and institution, you may also be able to create a mailing list for an e-newsletter about future instruction opportunities or general library news or a follow-up survey about their satisfaction with and perceived benefits from library instruction. Again, you would want to respect students' identities and preferences, distributing messages without revealing their information to others while also providing an easy method for them to opt out of future contact of this sort.

ASSESSING YOUR MARKETING

Gauging the success of your marketing plan for online workshops can be tricky. If you post flyers with tear-away information sheets, you can check in on them periodically to see how many have been taken. If you create a print or digital poster with a QR code to more information (or session registration), you can track how many times it is scanned. We use Delivr's free tool to create and track QR codes; however, our statistics show almost no QR code use by our populations in the almost two years we have tracked them.[6] Another free and easy way (with a Google account) to track both link clicks and QR scans is to enter the original URL in Google's link shortener.[7] It not only tracks total clicks and clicks by date but also the browser, platform, referrer, and country of each visitor (anonymously). If you choose to utilize social media, you can watch for trends in views and shares on Facebook, Twitter, and Instagram. If you use YouTube to share recordings of your videos, you can check for views on those as well as see for how long people watch, at what point they tend to quit, and whether they repeat any particular segment. We will discuss assessment of the content itself and provide more details on tracking link clicks and video views in chapter 9.

Of course, the fact that twenty people liked your event on Facebook or hearted your session promo image on Instagram does not mean those twenty people will show up to your session. There may indeed be some link or correlation between gains in social posts and session attendance, but the social media is in no way the definitive cause of that larger audience. One easy way to get an actual causation measurement of the impact of your marketing activity is to ask session attendees how they heard about the session. This simple, one-question quiz can be multiple choice and present the avenues you have chosen for marketing as well as options for word of mouth and, if permitted by your survey capabilities, an "other" field where responders can fill in the blank. Administering this should take less than thirty seconds and can be accomplished as part of students' introduction and orientation to the online classroom. If you use a registration system you can also include questions about where they heard about the workshop as they sign up for events. Using a newsletter program like MailChimp, you can also track how people read your marketing pieces sent via email.[8] For example, we sent a newsletter to a group of people and were able to note which links they clicked on and which they did not. This gave us an indication of what they found to be interesting and allowed us to think more about our offerings.

Obviously, attendance in the workshops can be another indicator of marketing success, but remember that this is only one of the results of the awareness campaign. So, even though your workshops may not be filled to capacity, by choosing to follow a carefully strategized marketing plan, you can still succeed in increasing awareness even if you do not see a dramatic rise in workshop participation. You might also consider distributing a survey to gauge awareness of library services and resources at the beginning of the semester and then redistribute at the end of the semester after your marketing plan has been implemented. This information can supplement any increase in workshop attendance and reinforce the idea that marketing, in and of itself, can be an effective tool for sharing information about the library.

IDEAS TO TRY

Let us close this chapter with some ideas that you can use, either directly or as a stepping stone in developing strategies specifically for your institution. Marketing online library workshops can manifest in many forms from print mailers to blog articles to Facebook posts. You also should note that marketing can happen through events and contests.

- Set up a series of online workshops and offer a library incentive to any student who attends three or more sessions. This prize could be anything from a t-shirt to a library bookmark. Keep in mind that you may want something that could survive being mailed to off-campus students.
- Use online workshops as a platform to launch some peer tutoring. Ask if interested students want to remain in the online classroom or meet in a Google Hangout to discuss their research projects after the session is over.
- Create a brief video that could be used as a vlog (video blog) post on the university or library webpage that talks about your online workshops.
- If you have on-campus students taking your online sessions, offer a chance to "Win a Study Room" during exam week for attending online workshops.
- Offer library prize packs for students or faculty who mention online workshops on their own social media accounts.
- Send a print mailer to all teaching faculty with a list of online workshops that will be provided throughout the semester. The irony may get their attention if nothing else!

No matter what you try with marketing your online sessions, the important thing to remember is to keep trying! Some things will work really well and others will fail spectacularly. Either way, you will get the library and its services out to a broader audience and learn the particulars of what does and does not work for your institution's unique culture.

NOTES

1. "Color Contrast Checker," *WebAIM*, accessed November 3, 2015, http://webaim.org/resources/contrastchecker/.

2. Brian Mathews, "Marketing Today's Academic Library," *A Bold New Approach to Communicating with Students*, ALA Editions, 2009.

3. "Free Software from Springshare," *Springshare*, accessed November 3, 2015, http://springshare.com/free.html.

4. Calculated with Color Contrast Checker for normal-sized text based on default #222 font color.

5. "Clemson Event Calendar," *Clemson University*, accessed November 12, 2015, http://calendar.clemson.edu/.

6. "Manage and Track Campaigns Using Short URLs, QR Codes®, NFC Tags, and Beacons," *Delivr*, accessed November 3, 2015, http://delivr.com/.

7. "Google URL Shortener," Google, accessed November 3, 2015, https://goo.gl/.

8. "Send Better Email," MailChimp, accessed November 24, 2015, http://mailchimp.com/.

EIGHT
Reaching Out to Faculty

Faculty members are the gateway to students' attendance at library workshops, whether online or face-to-face. Your best bet for participation in the development of your online sessions is to get faculty involved early and for the instruction that you provide to be directly related to an assignment or course. For online workshops in particular, it is especially important to have faculty buy-in as this type of workshop can take more time to prepare than traditional workshops and you want to make sure that your instruction reaches students. In this chapter, we will explore some ideas that may help you increase faculty participation in planning and implementing online library workshops, but the main areas for faculty outreach include the creation of online programming from the library and then the efforts that you will need to make to begin having conversations with departments across campus.

MEETING YOUR FACULTY

Just as we introduced you to Jane Q. Student in chapter 1, we would like now to introduce you to two faculty members: Elizabeth T. Faculty and John T. Lecturer. Elizabeth is fully tenured, has been at Anywhere University for fifteen years and is well respected both in her department and on campus. She serves on the faculty senate and as a vice president for her national organization, all while teaching a full load of classes. Many of Elizabeth's courses are ones she has taught for a number of years and fulfill one of the university's general education requirements. She would like to make changes to her courses, but between her national and local obligations, she finds it difficult to carve out any time in which to attend sessions on new classroom technologies. Her level of scholarship is impressive and, in fact, she has just published a new book, so she feels quite confident in relaying the importance of scholarly materials to her students. When it comes time to grade her students' papers, she often finds herself a bit disappointed in the online sources they are using. Between grading, meetings, dealing with emails, and teaching, Elizabeth finds she is working almost sixty hours a week.[1] This leaves little time for professional development or thoughts of possible collaborations with librarians. However, Elizabeth might find a prepackaged online session about source evaluation handy to plug into her courses in the hopes of improving student assignments.

Allow us now to introduce John T. Lecturer. John is a new faculty member interested in making new connections. He is very interested in building partnerships and working toward his newly formed professional goals. His primary focus is teaching and he is coming into the job with a high level of comfort with the online instruction environment. In fact, John earned one of his degrees online and has a deep understanding of this classroom setting. As John plans to teach his first class in the fall semester, he will be actively seeking ways to build his professional persona on campus as well as plan his first classes and find what works well with his students. He has yet to become heavily involved in the administrative cogs of the campus and is still learning about the plethora of resources at his disposal. John and Elizabeth are both examples of strong faculty on campus that have similar needs from the library and its resources but differing approaches to reaching them in their various stages of their professional careers. This is especially true when trying to encourage faculty to incorporate online learning in their classes.

CREATING ONLINE PROGRAMMING

When it comes right down to it, online library instruction does not differ fundamentally from face-to-face instruction because you are still trying to convey knowledge and skills. One way that you might be able to engage faculty in these workshops might be to rebrand your library instruction. The concept of the "embedded librarian" is not new, nor does it necessarily mean that the embedding is taking place online, but it is possible to use this term to create a fresh perspective for faculty on your library instruction. For example, if you encapsulate your online library services (all of which are already offered) in a program called "The Embedded Librarian Program" and repackage it for faculty in a neat webpage or flier, you have an opportunity to create marketing materials and communications that advertise this "new" service. This kind of faculty engagement with librarians may be better received by newer faculty who can be more comfortable with the online environment. Here at Clemson, we created an Embedded Online Librarian program to support our newly defined Clemson Online efforts. We used the opportunity to present the fact that Clemson University librarians are

- dedicated to the success of Clemson Online and its students
- ready to provide general and course-specific help with information sources
- knowledgeable about social media ("web 2.0") integration in higher education
- comfortable with the Blackboard and Canvas LMS

We also explain ways that we can help both faculty and students by listing the resources the library provides for both groups.

You can also take the opportunity to show how librarians can become more involved in faculty sessions online via discussion boards, during online virtual office hours, and as guest presenters. Again, many libraries already provide these services, but in creating an actual program in which you can incorporate all of the library's online services in one easily accessible place, it can make it easier for faculty to see the importance of including online library instruction in their courses. Placing an emphasis both on how librarians can help students as well as faculty can only strengthen the awareness of library instruction as a whole. This kind of program also makes it easier for librarians to approach larger online teaching initiatives with neat talking points about how the library can be more involved in online learning by using terms and language understood by those moving into the online teaching environment.

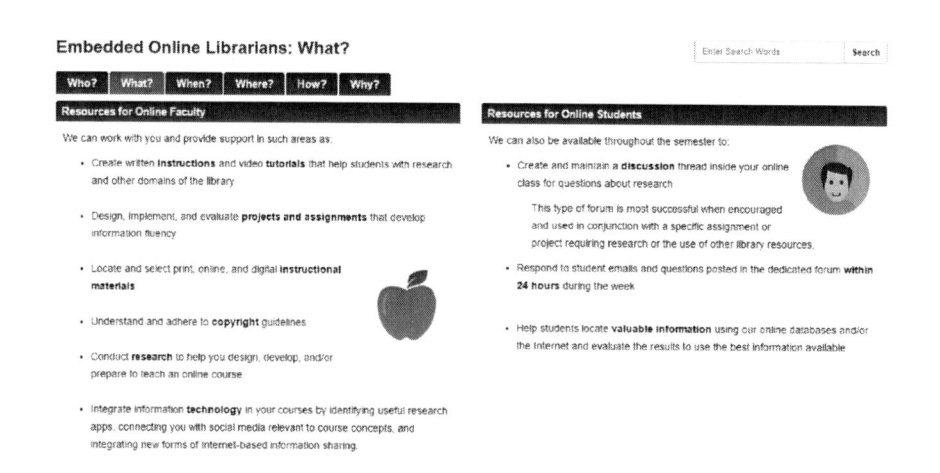

Figure 8.1. Description of Embedded Online Librarian

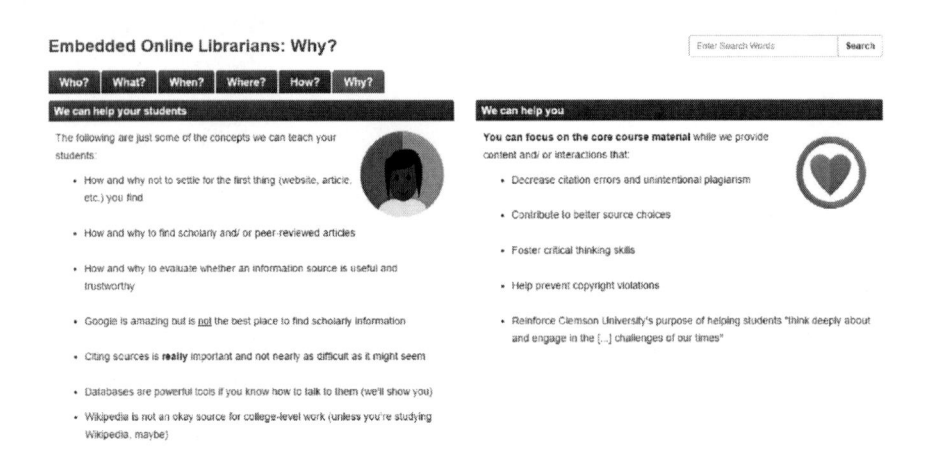

Figure 8.2. Role of Embedded Online Librarian

Seizing an Opportunity

One crucial aspect of librarian involvement in online instruction is responsiveness. Last fall, a teaching faculty member contacted our instruction coordinator about a problematic project turned in by a student who reused web content without attribution. The professor wanted confirmation that the student had been instructed on plagiarism and could be given a harsh punishment due to noncompliance. While there is indeed an official public statement about academic integrity and a set of procedures for addressing academic dishonesty, students received no general or foundational instruction about plagiarism, intellectual property, or attribution. While we do not know its outcome for the student, the case itself was a watershed for our presence within the online course for new students. It was apparent that students were being held responsible for this knowledge without having had a true chance to gain it. The topic is certainly an appropriate one for the library to address and as a part of a zero credit, required course for all incoming students, we already had a space in which to address this issue, so we created a tutorial to provide an introduction to the basic concepts.

We worked collaboratively to draft a script that clearly but concisely described plagiarism, its common forms, citations, and when to use them. Since the topic was conceptual, we used VideoScribe to create a fast-paced tutorial that was as engaging as possible. After creating the tutorial and five assessment questions that could be graded automatically within Blackboard, we asked for in-house volunteers to beta test the content. We had our seven brave volunteers watch the video and complete the quiz and then asked them to evaluate the questions' difficulty and provide any other feedback on the content as they felt necessary. Since we used

Qualtrics (more on that in chapter 9), we were able to measure the time each participant spent on the quiz portion. We wanted to make sure the quiz could be completed with knowledge gained from the video and that the content was not too difficult or too time-intensive. Of course, we readily admit the flaw in asking information-savvy library personnel to feign no prior knowledge of the topics covered. Our second step in testing was to release the content spring 2015 since only transfer students—approximately three hundred—take the course then versus the usual fall audience of more than four thousand. Having noticed no problems and received no negative feedback, we kept the content as is for the fall 2015 semester.

LIBRARIANS AS ONLINE EVENT PLANNERS

The promotion of online library workshops for faculty can also take place at events hosted or coordinated by the libraries. On many campuses, the library is considered the center for research materials, but with some concerted effort, it can also become the center for research sharing and discussion. The involvement of the online component can also be a natural extension of this as some libraries have also become centers for technology and digital maker spaces. Librarians should begin to take advantage of this situation and focus on the ways that online library instruction can enhance student (and even faculty) learning and research. Librarians can become leaders in group discussions about online learning and technology. As with the many other subjects for which we serve as liaisons, we do not necessarily need to be the experts in the field of online instruction and technology, but we can serve as the connection point between faculty and the resources that they need to learn more about teaching in the online environment. Then, during these facilitated discussions, librarians can promote their own online instruction, including online workshops on both general and specific research skills.

Specific examples of events that could be hosted by the library are discussed in the following sections.

Teaching and Researching with Technology

Reach out to those who work on campus in technology training as well as those who work with teaching effectiveness and offer to provide space and the addition of your expertise on finding resources and technology tools in the library to create an event that will highlight tools that faculty need to teach effectively online. This can create a "one-stop-shopping" effect that will appeal to faculty who have little time to spare, but who need a lot of information as they prepare to teach online.

Highlight Existing Online Teaching

Use the library to invite faculty members who are already teaching online to come in and share their experiences with others. Perhaps this could be a faculty member who effectively uses eReserves and might be willing to talk to other faculty about the benefits of this service.

Celebrate Open Access and National Distance Learning Weeks

Use these established annual events to provide a series of online or even face-to-face workshops that highlight librarians' expertise in this area of prime importance to any faculty member, but especially for those who may teach online. There may already be groups on your campus that host events for these occasions or at least departments that would be interested in sharing the spotlight (and their existing faculty connections) with you. Since these events take place during October and November, you may need to do some careful resource planning to carve out time in your otherwise busy fall semester.

Any of these events will provide an opportunity for librarians to talk to faculty about the role of library instruction in the online environment. In some cases, faculty have not considered including the library in their online instruction because they did not know that it was possible. Increased communication increases the possibility of faculty involvement in this innovative form of library instruction.

LIBRARY INFOMERCIALS

Another avenue for faculty outreach is via other workshops they are choosing to attend. For example, every college and university campus has technology instruction for faculty and these sessions would be an ideal place for the library to advertise online workshops. This could happen with the distribution of fliers before, during, or after sessions offered on topics about the use of the Blackboard, sessions on teaching with technology, or even a session on using Excel. If other trainers are particularly amenable, you could even provide a short video advertising a library service or your online workshops. In exchange, you can offer to advertise their workshops before, during, or after your library presentations. This kind of cross-pollination of faculty training can be particularly useful on campuses where training is dispersed rather than centralized. Many times, all it takes is a conversation with other trainers to learn that they would be more than willing to help you if you can help them as well.

Along the lines of taking your library instruction to the places where faculty members are already present, you may want to think about some other opportunities to insert information about online library training.

Could you ask your computer training group to mention library training opportunities if you send them a list of upcoming sessions? Does your campus have an office focused on innovation in teaching for faculty? At Clemson, we have the Office of Teaching Innovation and Effectiveness (OTEI) that provides face-to-face and online sessions geared toward professional development for faculty. You can connect with this office to provide sessions about library resources, services, and advanced research skills that could inspire more conversations about course integrated teaching. As mentioned in our chapter about marketing, it can be difficult for librarians to think of ways to push our training as this is new territory for us, but the time has come for a more thoughtful approach to our awareness campaigns.

WE RESERVE THE RIGHT TO CONTACT YOU

Almost every college or university campus library has a reserves program and within it there is some sort of online or paper form that a faculty member must fill out in order to place items in the system for student use. Library instructors can use this form to engage with faculty by creating a place on the form where faculty can request to be contacted by their subject librarian to set up a class or to create a research guide for their students. As shown in the screenshot excerpt, our current form has a check box near the bottom for them to opt in to this service.

You can make this request as descriptive as you like by offering opportunities not only to create online guides but also options to request other online instruction service. You could include the option to schedule online or embedded sessions or even request brief tutorials on a certain database that could then be posted within their course or electronic syllabus. Library reserves themselves also offer opportunities for embedding libraries in courses. At Clemson, our course reserve services now include the option to create live links in faculty syllabi to articles and eBooks. Now, all a faculty member has to do is submit their syllabus and our reserves coordinator creates links to items to which we have access and creates access to those we do not. This process has been made even easier for faculty as our library recently began using the reserves module in Springshare's LibGuides system. Previously, we had used the content management system, Blackboard, to upload course reserves into the institutional content section that was buried at least four clicks into the learning management system. This created a barrier for students and faculty alike when it came to accessing their course materials. Since the move to Springshare, course reserves can be linked to directly from the course page or even sent out via email from the faculty member. The use of library eReserves can be another online learning opportunity as tutorials and online sessions can be provided to encourage faculty to utilize this

Items for Reserve

Click the plus to add additional rows. Please key in only one item per row. Title and call number are required when requesting Library materials. Title is required for faculty owned material.

Call #	Title/Citation	Link (eReserve use only)

Are you interested in having an online guide to library resources for your class?

☐ Yes, please have my Subject Librarian contact me!

Reserve Acknowledegment *

☐ You will receive an email notification when your Reserves are available for student use. Allow 24-48 hours for processing. eReserves requiring copyright permissions are subject to addtional processing time.

[Submit]

Figure 8.3.   Course Reserve Request Form

essential service so that they avoid any copyright infringements in sharing research with their students. Clemson is not the only university to begin to make customer-friendly changes to their reserves system. Salisbury University in Maryland created new service models based on user feedback and included their reserve system in these changes.[2] Librarians at Seton Hall University found that the utilization of the LibGuides course reserve system was a successful solution to their quest to make their reserves more easily accessible. In fact, they found a 142 percent increase in usage of their eReserves system as a result.[3] This kind of improvement in library reserve service, whether print or online, can lead to more faculty involvement in library instruction based on their positive experiences. Course reserves can be a good avenue to find faculty who are already utilizing some library services but who might not know about the benefits of further collaborations with librarians.

MAXIMIZING THE LIBRARY LIAISON RELATIONSHIP

On campuses where subject liaison programs already exist within the libraries, these existing relationships can be leveraged to build online library instruction programming. A 2012 study from the University of North Carolina Greensboro has shown the shift in moving from a collection focus for subject liaisons to an instructional concentration and more specifically an instructional focus targeted toward faculty.[4] Almost any library with a subject liaison program will offer opportunities to intro-

Reaching Out to Faculty 107

duce the subject liaison using webpages specifically targeted to different research areas.

These pages can be used for promoting online instruction by providing

- Links to examples of online instruction
- Tutorials
- Recordings of past sessions

and by informing faculty of opportunities for course integration in the online environment

- Course reserves
- Online sessions
- Links to the online library classroom
- Promoting the online library event calendar
- Providing opportunities to live chat with subject liaison about research

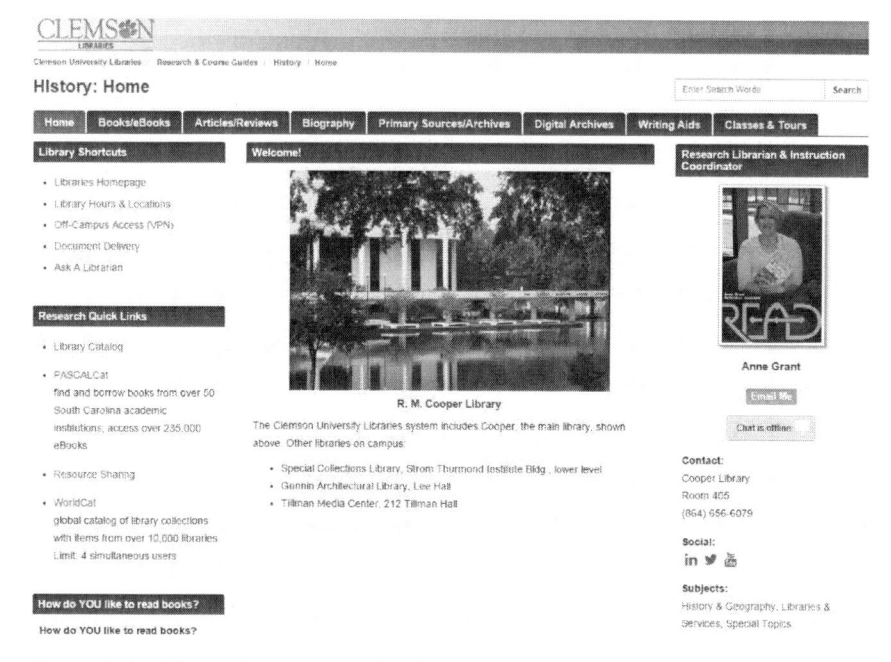

Figure 8.4. History Research Guide Homepage

These pages can be a key location to market subject instruction to faculty, whether face-to-face or online.

Subject liaisons can also do one-on-one outreach to faculty to gauge interest in instruction collaboration by setting up meetings with faculty in their departments. Instruction coordinators can supply a question bank that can be used to gather information and guide conversations. These questions could be divided into two sections with one for discussions about conducting research and the other about teaching. Some ideas for questions include:

Research

- Can you tell me a bit more about your current area(s) of research/interest?
- What are your go-to resources?
- What do you think students need to know about doing research? What should/do they already know about doing research?
- Does the library have the content you need to teach your classes and conduct research in your field? If not, what do you do? Whom do you communicate with when you have suggestions for new content?
- Research metrics are important for institutions with faculty research expectations. How do you share your research? How do you gauge how many people are viewing/using your research?
- How do you keep pace with new methods of scholarly communication such as portals, electronic portfolios, social media, web/cloud based platforms? Altmetrics?
- To what extent are you collaborating with peers in your research? What is the nature of your collaboration? What methods, software, platforms, or other mechanisms do you use to collaborate?

TEACHING

- How do you find and evaluate materials you use for teaching? Are librarians included in this process? If so, how? If not, why not?
- How do you teach and develop research skills the students need to complete your assignments?
- Describe a recent interaction with a student who was working on a research assignment. How did you guide the student's research?
- Do you have a process in place to guide students toward course- or assignment-related material and primary sources? If so, what is it?
- How do you evaluate student products that require scholarly resources? What weaknesses do you observe in student research? What are the strengths? Are you satisfied with resources students are using?
- List the library resources and services you use. Which are online? Which do you prefer to do in person at the library? Which would you like to have access to that is not currently available? Would you use instructional tutorials?

Once individual meetings have taken place, the qualitative data that was gathered can be used collectively to make changes to library services and to instruction. It can also provide valuable information about how receptive faculty are (or are not) to online library instruction initiatives.

THE BIG SWITCH: SUBJECT INSTRUCTION MOVES ONLINE

Traditionally, librarians have offered face-to-face sessions for the faculty in their subject areas. This process might involve a faculty member contacting a librarian with whom they have either worked before or may have heard of from a colleague and then setting up a time for the librarian to come to their class and lead a session on in-depth research in that subject. These sessions usually are assignment based and students come in with a particular goal in mind that will work toward a project completion. Helping faculty to think outside of this traditional library instruction box can be difficult, but providing clear options and helping them to understand how easy it is to integrate library instruction into either their face-to-face or online class can increase their involvement with subject liaisons. It may also help faculty to understand that asking a librarian to provide instruction to improve student research does not have to take up an entire face-to-face class session. This instruction can happen in the form of a tutorial or a live session that takes place during or outside of the normal class meeting time. These sessions can also be geared toward a particular database or other research tool that students will use for a course related project. This creates a just-in-time instruction tool that students can access as they are completing their project and have questions about how to best complete their assignment.

Ways to Provide Subject Instruction Online

- Librarian online hours—times in which subject liaison is available to chat online
- Database tutorials—brief sessions recorded in the online library classroom to discuss the use of subject related databases
- Live online sessions—online classes designed to assist student with specific projects or assignments
- Recorded online sessions—allows students to have access to past sessions that may help them with assignment completion

If your institution hosts a voluntary or mandatory syllabus repository, take the initiative to explore this valuable tool for staying aware of student assignments. Even if faculty do not contact you directly about curriculum-driven library collaboration, you will have an idea of the kinds of assignments students are being asked to complete and will have a better chance of creating online learning resources that will be useful. For example, as a part of the Quality Enhancement Plan that emerged from a recent Southern Association of Colleges & Schools (SACS) accreditation visit, Clemson began a Clemson Thinks program to improve students' critical thinking skills. As a part of this plan, professors revised existing course assignments to meet critical thinking guidelines and their refocused courses were tagged with a special indicator in the course catalog. Our instruction coordinator chose one of the courses within her subject area to investigate; she looked it up in the syllabus repository, read the assignments, and worked with our instructional designer to create a tutorial that would address critical thinking skills in the context of a particular assignment. We sent the tutorial draft to the professor (via a YouTube link), who responded after some delay with a couple of suggestions. We immediately made the recommended changes, prepared the video for public distribution, and let the professor know it was ready for incorporation in the course. While we would love to say this interaction was the beginning of strong collaboration, the reality since the final notification to the faculty member of the tutorial's completion, there has only been one view recorded on YouTube. This indicates that the faculty member did not use it in her course unless she showed it to them during a class session, but that seems unlikely. Along these same lines, you can also look at your course catalog for upcoming and recent semesters to identify classes that are completely or partially online (e.g., hybrid). These would be ideal candidates for online library learning pieces and you could contact the faculty teaching these sessions directly to open or bolster lines of communication and offer your online instruction services.

Your institution should have a group or governing body that reviews suggested course additions and modifications. In the best case, a library representative would be invited to serve on that group and could serve as an advisor for integrating library resources and information literacy concepts in all courses. At our institution, we are able to have a library representative attend curriculum committee meetings but only as an observer. Simply being present at and privy to what goes on at these meetings allows us to keep our figurative finger on the pulse of educational innovation at the university. Knowing which professors are proposing what courses means we can identify not only relevant ways to integrate our services but also the most appropriate and invested contact for hearing our pitch. In working on curriculum updates, these faculty members have indicated they are open to change; hopefully, this will at least somewhat correlate with a willingness to establish or increase the integration of library resources and instruction. Of course, it is important to keep in mind that much like our fictional professor, faculty are already busy with their current obligations but also going the extra mile to develop new courses. As such, they may not appear to be very responsive or even receptive to library collaboration. Make your pitch clear and your instruction as easy as possible to incorporate. Do not expect them to add a graded assignment or invite you in for an entire class period. Instead, offer ways you can help students succeed with an existing assignment. If there are no assignments for which library instruction would be a reasonable fit, perhaps you can provide instruction about existing resources that could help students accomplish their course or career goals. For example, students in a class with a collaborative assignment may benefit from a tutorial on finding eBooks about successful group work. Similarly, students in a theater class may benefit from a tutorial about searching current jobs in performing arts and information about the recording technology available for checkout.

There are also opportunities to contact faculty via faculty senate meetings or via online programming that already exists. Institutions that already have organized online programming have the perfect audience for promoting online library instructional opportunities and every institution has bodies of the faculty, such as a faculty senate, that meet regularly and would provide platforms for introducing online library instruction components. If librarians are members of the faculty at your institution, you will have representatives on this group who can also serve as a voice and a connection point for library collaboration with teaching faculty. Additionally, many subject liaisons have access to departmental meetings to both gather ideas for creating online learning pieces and for opening doors to future conversations about integrating library instruction into existing courses. For example, our education reference librarian once had the opportunity to speak at an orientation for new PhD students but was unable to go in person due to a scheduling conflict. We created a short recording that included both video to introduce the subject liaison and screen capture to show the library webpage and sent the completed project to the lead faculty member, who shared it with the students. As a result, our librarian experienced more individual student contacts with this video than we ever had with the face-to-face sessions. Students indicated that they were pleased with the video and were able to go back and watch parts that they had missed initially.

Involving faculty in online library instruction is crucial to its success. The earlier you can make contact with faculty when building online pieces the better, as early contact allows you to create pieces that will directly respond to student needs and will offer the additional benefit of being endorsed by the faculty who are teaching their courses. The more you try these environments, the more comfortable and adaptable you will become. It helps to remember that many faculty members are learning about online teaching right along with you.

NOTES

1. Colleen Flaherty, "So Much to Do, So Little Time," *Inside Higher Ed.*, April 9, 2014, https://www.insidehighered.com/news/2014/04/09/research-shows-professors-work-long-hours-and-spend-much-day-meetings.

2. Mou Chakraborty, Michael English, and Sharon Payne, "Restructuring to Promote Collaboration and Exceed User Needs: The Blackwell Library Access Services Experience," *Journal of Access Services* 10, no. 2 (2013): 93.

3. Sharon Ince and John Irwin, "LibGuides CMS eReserves: Simplify Delivering Course Reserves through Blackboard," *Interlending & Document Supply* 43, no. 3 (2015): 147.

4. Jo Henry, "Academic Library Liaison Programs: Four Case Studies," *Library Review* 61, no. 7 (2012): 492.

NINE
Assessing Online Instruction

Keeping track of online learning can be a bit more challenging than tracking traditional face-to-face sessions. This is true both in numbers of attendees as well as the ability to gather feedback about content. There are many ways that assessment data can be gathered for both face-to-face and online sessions and this chapter will cover the ways that we here at Clemson have tried to collect responses to our instruction so you will have an idea about tools and methods that can be used in gathering data. Most of the information gleaned from the tools we describe can be considered what is known as alternative metrics, or nontraditional methods of evaluating impact and audience engagement. This kind of data can accentuate the more traditional national statistical data gathered by groups like the Association of Research Libraries, who continue to quantify instruction by numbers of sessions held and number of attendees. Numbers for online instruction can be harder to pin down since you are counting both those who attend the live session as well as those who may watch the recording at a later time. Likewise, if you create a tutorial, you need to make sure that you can gather statistics on how many people viewed your content. When hosting videos in-house on a local server, you may need to request access or download data from your information technology department. For example, Vimeo, a video hosting service, allows you to access weekly view statistics but requires a paid account upgrade for more view information such as country of viewer or site on which the video watched is embedded. Overall, assessing an online program for both number of attendees and content can be achieved by documenting efforts and attendance, creating feedback opportunities, and by completing the cycle of feedback.

SURVEY TECHNOLOGIES

Much like with online classroom technology, your institution may already offer a solution for creating and distributing feedback surveys. We recommend you inquire whether there is someone knowledgeable about survey technology and best practices. If not, your library or institution may at least have an institutional account or a service recommendation. In case your inquiries have left you completely to your own devices, we will discuss three survey options and some of their main features and drawbacks. You may know of additional free options we do not cover, but we picked those with which we had the most experience.

Google Forms

As with other Google services, you need only a Google account and there are no paid account options or upgrades. Display logic is available for multiple choice and "choose from a list" question types by selecting the "Go to page based on answer" check box. Within the advanced settings of text entry fields, you can choose data validation for URL or email address or set your own criteria. Of the approximately twenty free features available in the add-ons menu, there are a few that could be especially useful for survey power users. Form notifications allow you to send yourself (or someone else) an email after every x responses are received. It also provides the ability to send an automatic email to each respondent; the subject line and plain text body content will be the same for all messages. Another useful add-on, formLimiter, can close your survey at a certain date, time, or response quantity.

If you want your surveys to reflect your institutional identity (and you should), Google Forms offers a generous amount of flexibility in colors, borders, and the font, size, and color of text. There are twenty font options listed and scores more available if you enjoy suffering from decision paralysis. Of course, all these options mean you are now responsible for ensuring the resulting survey represents your library well and has appropriate color contrast for accessibility (see chapter 7). You can customize any of the approximately twenty-five default themes, starting with the blank canvas of the basic theme or choosing something more festive such as "Birthday Cats" or "Library." If you want to benefit from a theme but avoid the instant giveaway that you have used a free Google form, we recommend changing the survey's main image. After selecting a theme, the Customize link will appear; the Choose Image button is at the top of that menu. Google offers a considerable library of preformatted images that are organized into ten categories. Google Forms is a service for all types of users, so there are banners for weddings, major and minor holidays, and children's birthday parties. The best categories to check for professional, "library-ish" images are Illustrations (scrolling past the clovers and ghosts) and Other. It is worth noting that the options provided by Google include both static and animated images. Depending on which images you have displayed, this may not be readily apparent and, for some viewers, the images with subtle movement can be a little unsettling or off-putting. There is currently no way to filter or display only one type. Since some of the motion is quite subtle, the quickest method to identify the animated GIFs is to hover on the image and pay attention to the file type suffix listed in the tooltip. The static images seem to all be JPGs. In true Google fashion, it is also easy to use an image from your Google albums and Drive or upload one just for this. If you make your own, use a four to one ratio (W:H) and aim for six hundred pixels in width.

SurveyMonkey

This is a well-known choice for creating free surveys, probably because its 1999 birthday makes it practically an old-timer in the Internet world. A free account can be created via linking to Google or Facebook. Unless you maintain those accounts exclusively for professional use, though, you should probably go ahead and create a separate account with your institutional email. SurveyMonkey works on a freemium business model in that its basic service is free but advanced features are not. With a free account, you can create at least fifteen surveys up to ten questions in length and collect up to one hundred responses per survey. If you get more than one hundred responses to a survey and want to access them, you must upgrade to a professional (AKA paid) account. If you exceed a thousand responses in a month, you will pay some more. These limitations are clearly stated, but one of the worst parts about SurveyMonkey is its unclear delineation between free and paid features. There are a dozen color schemes available; the "customize theme" option appears as a normal menu item but leads only to a pop-up promoting an account upgrade. Nestled between two other options in the "Analyze Results" area is the "Data Trends" tab, another pop-up generator. While these pop-ups are at least modern, in-window notifications, they make it very frustrating until you have learned exactly which of the regular-seeming options are off-limits. In summary, you may be using Survey-Monkey based on momentum or popular recommendation, but there are now better free options.

Qualtrics

At Clemson University Libraries, we have single-account access to Qualtrics Research Suite. One employee and one backup are able to create, access, and manage our surveys. Because of Qualtrics' advanced security and survey features, we are able to use it for surveys that have both internal and external audiences. The ability to upload an email distribution list and send a unique survey link to each recipient has two main benefits. The first is that each recipient can respond only once, removing the possibility of "stuffing" the figurative survey box. The second is that each response is from someone who should have an informed opinion about the survey topic. The standard distribution method for Google Forms and SurveyMonkey is one based on a central link. Anyone that gains access to it can respond and, depending on other settings, may find it easy to respond multiple times (whether intentionally or on purpose). While it is rare that a student may tweet your survey link or post it on Reddit, this is a potential source of error that must be acknowledged in any results analysis.

As you may have deduced, the level of Qualtrics we use is not free. Pricing information is by individual request from Qualtrics, likely because it depends on factors such as student or employee population; therefore, we are not able to discuss pricing information as it might relate to your particular institution and needs. Unlike Google, Qualtrics is a business with surveys and analytics at its core. As such, they are not in the business of making all their survey features available as with Google Forms. However, Qualtrics is the survey method we use and are most familiar with, so we wanted to include it in this section on survey tools. Since we realize that some of our readers may not have funds available for a dedicated survey solution, we investigated their free account so we could discuss its viability as an option. It is limited to one active survey, which means only one form can be used to collect data at any given time, and this survey can only collect up to one hundred responses. Available features include standard question types, basic reporting, and some survey customizations such as display logic, looping, and question order randomization. Survey branding and HTML customization are not available with a free account. For a small library or one with a specialized survey need, Qualtrics' free account may be worth exploring. While it will likely be insufficient for any comprehensive assessment program, you may want to use it if you face the need for privacy and audience restrictions that are not available from other free survey services.

ASSESSING LIVE SESSIONS

Counting attendees is the easiest way to get some data about your session. If you collect no other data, this is it. While we do not want to give the impression that counting attendees in the virtual classroom is difficult, we do want to note a few unique aspects. In-person attendance is generally taken at the beginning of a session. Also, it is obvious if a student leaves during the session, which makes it easy for the instructor to make a snap judgment about whether the student was present long enough to be counted as a legitimate attendee. Barring a simple miscount or tallying error, there is no risk of counting a student more than once. In the online classroom, counting attendees requires you to be aware of several ways your "head count" may differ. To get an accurate count, instructors should know the answer to these questions before the session begins:

- At what point is attendance taken?
- Do we need just a tally of attendees or should I check them against registrations?
- How can I tell if a student is logged in more than once?
- Do we admit students after the session begins? How late can they be and still be counted (and have it count if they are there for class credit)?
- If you have more than one instructor (or a classroom assistant), which person is responsible for taking attendance?
- Do I report this the same way as in-person instruction or not?

While some of the above are indeed relevant to the physical classroom, the answers for the brick-and-mortar classroom may be taken as a given. If the online environment is new or new to an instructor, not answering these questions ahead of time may mean your attendance data is not as accurate as it should be or not collected at all. After all this, you may say to yourself, "It's just attendance! What's the big deal?" Attendance data is expected and ubiquitous. It seems so straightforward and definite that it can carry a lot of weight when one looks at instruction trends, especially if looking at them from above (in an administrative capacity). Attendance data is absolutely an important piece of the puzzle, especially when gauging return on investment in terms of total students reached. However, attendance is the tip of the iceberg for instruction sessions, and we will discuss multiple other ways to track and quantify your teaching efforts. Gathering feedback from participants as they complete sessions or groups of sessions can also provide valuable feedback. At Clemson, we provided session evaluations for our Graduate Student Boot Camp series and another series of workshops geared toward graduate students at George Mason University were also evaluated with changes made based on feedback from participants.[1]

Counting Reference Questions

When leading a live session, what you are going to cover and what all you actually cover may be very different. This is especially true if you end up with a small audience or even an ad hoc one-on-one consult. Depending on how your library keeps statistics on reference interactions, you may want to keep track of any questions you get during the session and any question and answer period at the end. Recording the questions you get can help you refine your session, prepare other instructors that might cover this content, and quantify the extra effort you put into teaching that session to "just" one or two students.

From Registrant to Attendee

If you are using a session registration system that collects student identifiers, you have the ability to identify a unique demographic. By comparing your list of registrants with your actual attendees, you can identify those students who sign up but do not attend. If you have the time and resources during a session, you may want to reconcile those lists then. Otherwise, you can compare them after the fact. Comparing them after the session will also allow you to identify students that only attend part of the session. What you do with this information depends on your available staffing power and decisions you make about what fits within your campus culture. You may want to generate a standard follow-up email for students that register but do not attend. This should be crafted with care and perhaps even reviewed briefly by any available student workers or volunteers you have at your disposal. The goal is to be informative and helpful, not come across as judgmental, overbearing, or attempting to guilt them for not attending. The tone of the email will of course depend on your campus culture and the communication norms and standards set forth by your library.

> Subject: Recent Library Instruction Session
> Dear [student],
> We noticed that you recently signed up for our [class name] session but were unable to attend. No worries! We just want to make sure this wasn't due to trouble with our classroom technology. If you did encounter any difficulty with our online classroom, we would appreciate it if you'd {let us know}. If you're still interested in this or other library topics, we have {more sessions} coming up this semester plus a selection of {online tutorials}.
> Best wishes from [library name]!

If you want to create a simple survey and email it to registrants that did not attend, you can substitute in some text about that, such as, "If you could take a few seconds and {complete our anonymous survey} why you didn't attend, we'd really appreciate it." The text in curly brackets could link to a one-question multiple-choice survey such as,

I didn't attend this session because I . . .

- forgot about it.
- had a schedule conflict.
- decided I wasn't interested or didn't need it.
- had trouble with the online classroom.
- Other:

If you want to comment on your response, you can {email [contact]}.

Listening to Your Participants

Building an evaluation form into the closing of your online session will allow your students to provide feedback while it is still fresh on their minds. If you are unable to do this (or forget as we occasionally do), collecting attendees' email addresses means you can send it out to them as soon as the session ends. If you go this route, we want to remind you (one more time) to use BCC instead of listing the addresses for all to see to protect the privacy of attendees. You can gauge anything from confidence in library skills to rating actual research ability in these surveys, but you will most likely want to gather information about what was helpful to those who attended and what they might still like to see more information about. These tools can also be used to help determine the application of library skills by asking attendees to let you know what skill they learned in your session that they will use to apply to either the class they are in currently or an assignment on which they are working. By asking this kind of question, you can report about what percentage of those who attended your sessions will actively apply the skills you taught them to their academic work. The same is true for asking about confidence level because if you ask participants "After attending this library session, how confident do you feel about doing library research in general?" responses to this question will allow you to report percentages of confidence level that your session provided to attendees and can indicate library instruction's contribution to student and faculty success. As with any opportunity to interact with your attendees, you will want to make sure that you ask questions that will produce information you can use to continue to build your program. Always think about how you will use the information that you gather as you listen carefully to what your attendees have to say.

You will want to create as many opportunities for feedback as possible but make them as painless as possible. This means encouraging your instructors to have attendees complete evaluations after any type of instruction session, whether it be a presentation within an online class or a drop-in session in the library classroom. If your survey solution supports display logic, it is worth the effort to include it whenever you can to make the survey experience easier for your audience. By carefully planning the flow of your survey and using display logic, you can use one survey form to collect data on these multiple instruction types yet not subject your respondents to sets of questions they need to skip past or ignore. Since we use a little display logic in our workshop survey form, we decided to represent it as a flowchart. We adapted the established workflow shapes to fit our needs, using rectangles for multiple-choice questions, a double-ended arrow to indicate that the two questions below it provide standard Likert scales, and parallelograms to indicate free-text response fields.

Listening to Your Instructors

As you plan the move from face-to-face to online instruction, one group that can be easily overlooked when gathering information about library instruction sessions are the instructors themselves. If teaching online is new to your library, it is crucial that you keep your finger on the pulse of your instructors as they find ways to deal with the changes to their teaching style. One way to do this is through attending sessions and providing constructive feedback to instructors about their presentation, interaction, and content. You could also have instructors fill out self-evaluations using the same rubric or even provide opportunities for peer evaluation. It can be very easy to find yourself in a position where teaching librarians are all doing their own things and miss the opportunity to watch their colleagues and learn new ways to interact with students. Once you have gathered the data from either the self-evaluations or the peer evaluations, you can provide all instructors with a "Tips from the Field" sheet that collects some of the best teaching ideas and shares it among all instructors.

You can also ask for feedback from your instructors about the online classroom environment itself by asking questions like:

- Does the online classroom provide adequate opportunities to interact with students?
- Do you feel comfortable in the online classroom?

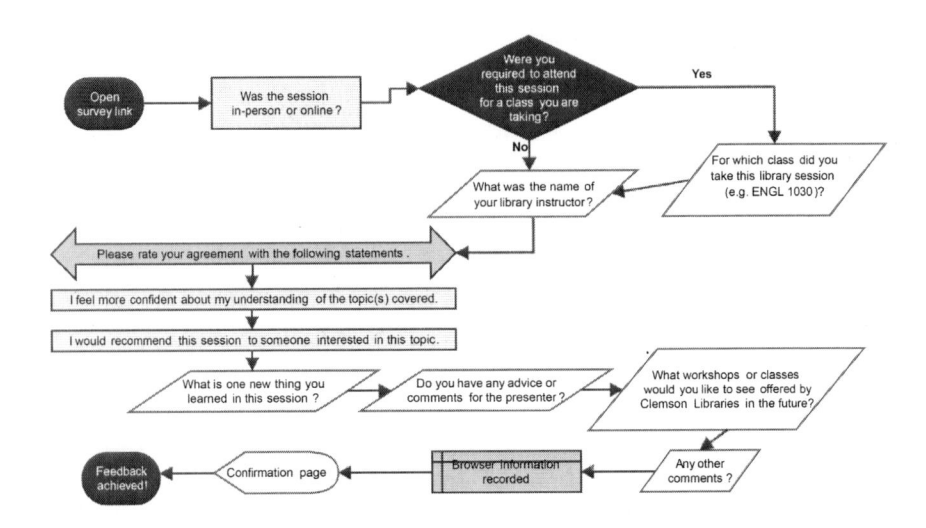

Figure 9.1.   Diagram of Instruction Session Feedback Survey

Assessing Online Instruction 121

	Unsatisfactory	Needs Work	Excellent
Delivery	• Audio is difficult to hear or understand	• Audio is mostly intelligible with limited quality issues	• Audio is clear and intelligible with no disruptions
	• Does not seem prepared and knowledgeable about topic	• Lacks some preparation or higher knowledge about topic	• Prepared and conveys good understanding of topic
	• Overall pace is rushed, dragging, or inconsistent	• Some sections are rushed, dragging, or inconsistent	• Pacing is consistent, appropriate for audience
	• Seems uncomfortable with or anxious about technology	• Shows some discomfort with or anxiety about technology	• Seems at ease with technology, any difficulties
Engagement	• Expresses no interest in or enthusiasm about topic	• Inconsistent or inauthentic interest in topic	• Conveys appropriate and consistent interest in topic
	• Does not explain input methods or solicit responses	• Incomplete explanation or limited calls for interaction	• Explains and encourages use of input methods
	• Ignores student input (e.g. chat/Q&A box, status icons)	• Delayed or absent in some responses to student input	• Responds appropriately to all input (may use assistant)
	• Does not launch survey	• Does not introduce survey, purpose, or expectations	• Introduces survey adequately before launch
Content	• Contains inaccurate or outdated information	• Some information or processes need updating	• Information and processes correct and up-to-date
	• Absent or unprofessional visuals	• Some poor-quality or inadequate visuals	• Visuals are high-quality and maintain brand identity
	• No source or copyright consideration given	• Insufficient credit or respect for intellectual property	• Appropriate consideration and credit given
	• Does not follow outline, objectives, or description	• Some disorganization or distraction from session plan	• Well-organized and focused content coverage
	• Examples are absent or show no understanding of audience	• Need additional or more relevant examples	• Well-timed examples are relevant for audience

Figure 9.2.   Online Instructor Evaluation Rubric

- What would make you feel more comfortable teaching in the online classroom?
- Did you encounter any technical difficulties while teaching online? If so, what happened?
- What do you feel worked really well when teaching in the online classroom?

Once you have the responses to questions like these, you can revisit your classroom space to make any improvements or adjustments. While gathering this kind of feedback can take time, it is well worth the investment as your instructors will feel more a part of the planning process and can take some ownership as their workshops shift in their format.

ASSESSING RECORDED CONTENT

Whether you provide a link to a recorded live session or create a tutorial, keeping statistics for asynchronous instruction is becoming more and more important as a library instruction metric. Your number one source of data on whether your audience is taking advantage of your online content is in the number of views the content receives online. With synchronous instruction, it is generally easy to know exactly how many attendees you have. With recorded content, one access or view could actually represent an instance when your content was used by a study group or shown to an entire class. There is generally no way to account for this except in the context of library instruction at your institution. To help capture the most accurate measurement of your true audience, you will want to build in a way to factor this kind of occurrence in when leading instruction sessions. For example, if one of your library instructors teaches a class and shows one of the library tutorials during their session, ask them to let your statistic keeper know when they showed the online piece and how many people were there to watch. This number (minus the one view each that actually *was* counted) can be added to the automatic view tally at the end of each semester or year.

While we had the opportunity to choose our video hosting platform, we recognize that other librarians may not be as fortunate. If you are institutionally or otherwise compelled to use a hosting solution that does not track views, you can still gather some automatic statistics on your work by passing your video URLs through a link shortener before distributing them to your audience. Based on our experience, we will discuss how to do this with Google's URL shortener.[2] If you already have experience or an account with one of the other link shorteners out there, you may want to skip ahead to the next paragraph. Requiring only a Google account (you have one by now, right?), this service includes excellent additional features. We would call them added-value but were unsure whether you can add value to an already free resource. For each URL you shorten, you will see a running tally of link clicks on the main page of the link shortener. By selecting "Details" on a row, you can see several more types of click information. The graph of clicks by date has display options for the past two hours, day, week, or month. You can also choose to view a graph of "all time," which has a data point for each month. There is no custom date option. There is also aggregated information on the link user's referrer, web browser used, country, and platform used. As a note, the referrer listed for almost all the links we have tracked with this service is "unknown." The URL shortener also automatically provides a QR code (dimensions 100px^2) and logs the link creation date so you know for sure when you started counting.

At this point, we want to take just a moment to remember (although it may seem obvious) that statistics tell us only what they tell us. To be precise, Google URL shortener tracks times your video was accessed, not times it was watched. With hosting systems that do track views specifically, it can be easy to assume that six hundred video views means six hundred people watched it. While it is likely that many people only watched it once (and that three hundred did not watch it twice or one person six hundred times), there could of course be those who watched it multiple times. Similarly, we want to remind those new to assessment that correlation is not necessarily causation. While you may notice an increase in video views after you promote your YouTube channel in a

Video Analytics on the YouTube Platform

At Clemson Libraries, we host our instruction and outreach videos on a YouTube channel. While view statistics were not among our primary reasons for choosing this platform, we were pleasantly surprised by the wealth of information available at no extra cost for our free account. Housed within YouTube's Creator Studio, the Analytics area provides preset time filters for weekly, monthly, quarterly, or yearly statistics plus the ability to set a custom date range. These filters can be used to refine the statistics displayed for individual videos, playlists, content comparisons, or the channel as a whole. If you want a snapshot of your tutorial efforts, the lifetime or time-period channel overview is excellent. Recognizing the timing of when students are accessing the content can be useful to determine future live sessions as well. Studies have found that instruction provided at the right time in an assignment cycle can have a greater impact.[3]

This screenshot shows the first two sections of the lifetime statistics for our channel. As you would imagine with aggregated data, all this view information is anonymous. Data for more personal interactions, such as shares, subscribers, and likes, are also anonymized. Hovering on

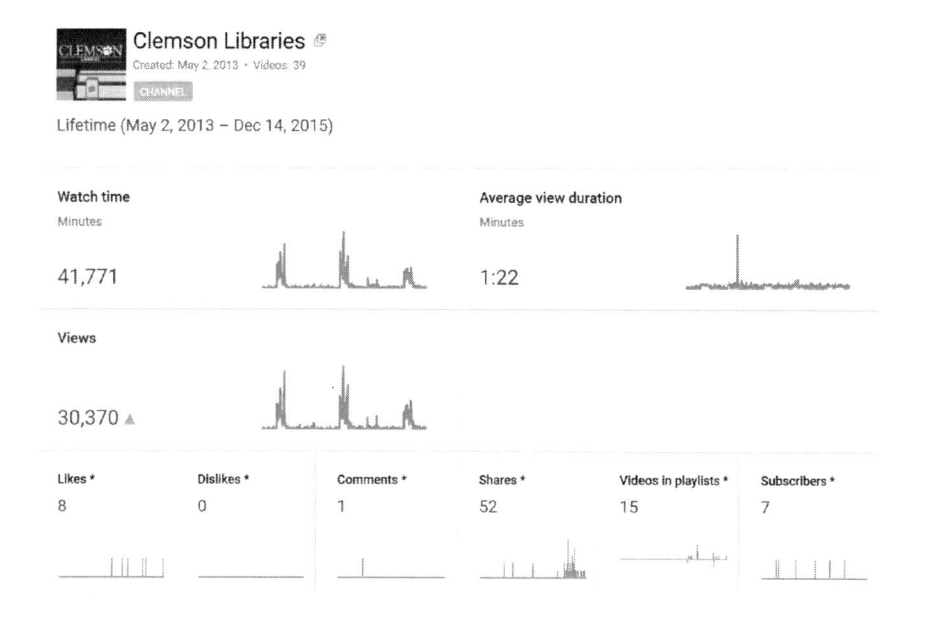

Figure 9.3. YouTube Channel Summary Statistics

some sections will sometimes provide more data, such as the dates of any intervals for which that statistic may not have been collected. Even these sections provide more data than you may need and certainly more than you would want to share without some corresponding explanations. You may wish to replicate only the data you wish to highlight or edit the screenshot to erase unnecessary sections. This is by no means an attempt to skew the data but rather to streamline what is presented. If you disable comments by default or do not use playlists, there simply may be no need to clutter the snapshot. It is worth noting that the video count, which is displayed at the top under the channel name, includes all videos currently in your account despite any time filters you have set. Not pictured, the next section of the channel overview is the list of top ten videos. Each row has columns with the video name (a hyperlink to the video's watch page), the total views and their percentage of all channel views, the estimated minutes watched and that percentage of all minutes watched, and the likes. Depending on your video retention policy and the included duration of the report, you may see one or more video names as "Unidentified video." Similarly, if you retain previous versions on your YouTube channel, your perspective on the lifetime of a video may require combining data from multiple rows.

Under "Top Geographies" is a list of the five countries with the most viewers and a small world map. By selecting that section, you can see qualitative data for the rankings as well as the full list of countries. Assuming our channel is anything like that of the typical U.S.-based educational organization, 99 percent of our views are from the United States; the rest of the "top five" countries each have less than fifty views, and the astonishingly long list of other countries of access ranges from Azerbaijan to Vietnam.

Top geographies
Watch time

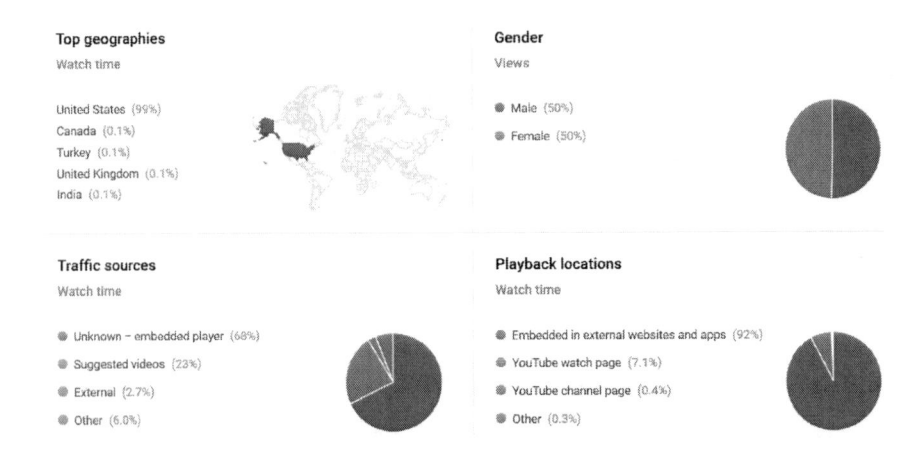

United States (99%)
Canada (0.1%)
Turkey (0.1%)
United Kingdom (0.1%)
India (0.1%)

Gender
Views

● Male (50%)
● Female (50%)

Traffic sources
Watch time

● Unknown – embedded player (68%)
● Suggested videos (23%)
● External (2.7%)
● Other (6.0%)

Playback locations
Watch time

● Embedded in external websites and apps (92%)
● YouTube watch page (7.1%)
● YouTube channel page (0.4%)
● Other (0.3%)

Figure 9.4. YouTube Channel Demographic Statistics

Unless you have the knowledge and resources to delve into statistical analysis, you will probably only use a small fraction of the data provided by YouTube. It can be easy to feel overwhelmed by the possibilities and the fact that exactly which segments of data you use will depend on what you are evaluating at that moment. Here are a few suggestions of what to do with some of the wealth of data that is available.

Devices

The type of device used by your viewers can help guide the type of video content you make and could even help your library technology personnel. When you look at these statistics, you may need to remind yourself how your videos can be accessed. If your videos are mostly available through embedding in information-intensive interfaces such as Blackboard, you will likely see far more computer users than mobile visitors. Device usage can also be directed by the content of the video. If the crux of its content is screen sharing, the mobile user may quickly abandon it.

Audience Retention

This information is very interesting when assessing individual videos for product improvement. YouTube provides graphs of absolute and relative audience retention, the former being a comparison with other videos (regardless of topic) of similar length. Is this video embedded and part of course content? If so, it makes sense that the audience retention levels will skew slightly higher because the viewers are a somewhat captive audience. Once again, it is important to remember that data is neutral. If viewers are given a quiz or assignment to hold them responsible for watching the video, you may notice spikes in the retention at the segment with those answers. You may also see a spike if there is a portion that viewers find particularly confusing or incomprehensible.

Caption Usage

Nested under the "Views" heading, data for subtitle and closed caption usage are available since May 11, 2014. Subtitles were used for the majority (as determined by YouTube) of 3 percent of all our views, which means that our captioning efforts were not wasted, as they were useful for almost six hundred views. In this case, these are instances of caption usage, which could be six hundred unique viewers, three hundred viewers that watched two videos each, or any other configuration thereof. By clicking the subtitle language, we are able to drill down into the country of our caption user and even the state for viewers within the United States.

FACULTY FEEDBACK

Another group vitally important to gauging the success of your online workshops is the teaching faculty who request library sessions. As librarians, we often get anecdotal feedback when a faculty member thanks us for the session and says that it was useful to their class, but in order to gather meaningful information that translates to annual instruction reports for the libraries, we must begin to take a more purposeful approach. This is especially true when moving from face-to-face to online instruction as the shift in format provides the perfect opportunity to collect feedback from faculty who request library instruction.

There are a couple of ways that you can request feedback from teaching faculty. You can ask for their qualitative personal satisfaction with the information provided as well as input on the online teaching platform. This is just a concerted effort to collect any comments faculty might have on the session and its value from each requested session instead of hoping that the faculty member takes the time to send in comments they might have on their own. While they may not all be faculty per se, now is a good time to consider soliciting feedback from any additional campus constituent with which you provided cooperative instruction. You can also ask whether they have any feedback mechanisms for which they can share the resultant data, assuming you are willing to do the same with yours.

You might also consider asking to collaborate with the faculty member on reviewing assignments that would be directly impacted by your instruction. For example, if the faculty member is asking you to provide a session to students about conducting library research to assist students in creating an annotated bibliography, ask if you might be able to review a random sampling of the student products. You could then use a rubric of some kind to gauge the quality of sources cited. You might also ask for grade comparisons to see if students who participated in library workshops or viewed library tutorials ended up with better grades in the course than those who did not.

At the end of each semester, many colleges and universities ask students to rate aspects of the course such as the instructor, difficulty, and content. This end-of-course survey is another excellent way to get feedback about your instruction efforts in a specific course. While it is technically a way to listen to your participants, we chose to include it here because of the librarian-instructor cooperation it involves. First, you must have established a relationship with the professor to allow you to include library instruction within their course. While this may be a synchronous session, it could also be the inclusion of one or more library tutorials in the course content or as part of a specific assignment. How course evaluations are conducted at your institution will determine the next step. It may be that you work directly with the professor to have your question(s) included in the course evaluation. For larger institutions, you may collaborate with a representative of the department that conducts and processes course evaluations. In either case, you will need the professor's consent to have your questions included on the course evaluation form. Finally, you need some way to receive the responses of the question(s) you included in the evaluation, which may require one-on-one work with the professor or the institutional research representative. While we have not yet used course evaluation questions to assess our online instruction, we did have that opportunity for face-to-face instruction; we will discuss that process in chapter 10.

DATA-DRIVEN CHANGE

Since each library will develop a unique online workshop program based on available resources, student needs, and instructor buy-in, the methods for applying assessment data will be equally individualized. We chose the following analysis areas because they will likely apply to many online workshop programs. If a suggestion is not relevant for your library, perhaps it will inspire you to seek related opportunities for applying your hard-earned assessment data to improving your instruction program.

Content Improvement

This is a broad category at the heart of why we solicit instruction feedback. Once you have done your foundational research (see chapter 3) and taken a bold first run at creating online workshop content, you will need to brace yourself and take a hard look at how you did. The primary data source for this type of change would be your student feedback surveys. Depending on how much effort you have been able to devote to assessment, you may also be guided by input from your library instructors and any campus faculty or departments with which you collaborated. As mentioned in chapter 3, there will almost always be someone that says what you have done is terrible; hopefully, these will be the outliers in your data. If these responses make up a significant percentage of the total, you have something to consider. Otherwise, these responses are really only useful should you receive the rare bit of harsh but well-reasoned criticism. Utilizing evaluation feedback to improve library instruction techniques is also important and can be done by providing participant feedback to instructors and creating one-on-one or group training opportunities for library instructors.

Return on Investment

In an occupation based on concepts such as ideas and knowledge, it can be almost impossible to answer the question of "Is it worth it?" with any conviction. However, your assessment data must help you balance how much effort you put into each instruction session, tutorial, and learning object with how much benefit there is for your students, faculty, and campus constituents. Unless you are the decision maker for or the sole recipient of library instruction responsibilities, the bigger decisions about return on investment will likely be made in consultation with your library administration. True to the abstract nature of much of librarianship, we are best equipped to provide some questions to help you determine where to focus your efforts and when to let things go.

- How many students do you need in a synchronous online session to make it worth doing?
- Is there a baseline response or participation rate for determining if you do a similar project again?
- Should you make an updated version of that video if only x people watched the first version?
- When do you make your own video and how do you count when you use someone else's?

SHOWING YOUR WORK

One of the most important things to remember when gathering assessment information is that you must always close the loop! Once data has been pulled together, it needs to be put into a report of some kind and presented to relevant groups. For instance, you will want to take information collected from your library instructors about the online teaching environment and show how you made changes to the learning environment based on their suggestions and comments. You may also find that you adjust what you offer based on your data gathered from students and teaching faculty. These changes can be something that you highlight to teaching faculty by letting them know that you made them based on their feedback and by notifying them that their feedback mattered, you can create a greater investment in their interest in library instruction.

Not only is it crucial to be able to translate this kind of instructional activity to national library data, but it is also vital that this form of instruction contribute directly to any university-wide planning and goals. Many colleges and universities are moving to improve access to classes and student support in the online environment, so it should not be difficult to find ways to align online library instruction with these sorts of goals. However, it is important to figure out ways to use the language of the university to help upper administration understand how this instruction fits into the larger goals. Therefore, not only are you working to get your library instructors on board, you are also working on gaining support from university administration. No pressure. This feedback is not only important in the larger picture, but it also creates opportunities within the group of teaching librarians in providing ways that they can show their effectiveness in teaching for performance evaluations and to document their contributions to the unit and the library as a whole. In a world where librarians are increasingly being asked to document their role in student success and retention, gathering this kind of feedback from the online teaching environment is crucial. You should also consider making sure that you share information you gathered that could help other areas within your library or institution. It is not your job to see that they effect change based on it, but your survey respondents and one-on-one contacts gave you that information in good faith, perhaps not even aware that the feedback was not specifically relevant to your instructional needs and should really have been presented elsewhere. In the end, remember that assessing an online program can be achieved by documenting efforts and attendance, creating feedback opportunities, and by completing the cycle of feedback.

NOTES

1. Roszkowski and Reynolds, "Assessing, Analyzing, and Adapting," 224–39.
2. "Google URL Shortener," *Google*, accessed November 3, 2015, https://goo.gl/.
3. Hilde Daland, "Just in Case, Just in Time, or Just Don't Bother? Assessment of One-Shot Library Instruction with Follow-Up Workshops," *LIBER Quarterly* 24, no. 3 (2015): 138.

TEN

Summing It Up

Tips, Sample Plans, and Fitting into the Big Picture

Setting out to make a change to your instruction program from a physical to an online environment can feel extremely overwhelming, but there is a great deal of information out there about others who have moved their training and educational opportunities online so you will not be forced to reinvent the wheel. While this book has included many ideas on how to begin movement of face-to-face instruction sessions online, this chapter will focus on some concrete lessons that we learned here at Clemson, clear examples of ways to incorporate online workshops, sample outlines and calendars, as well as plans for future directions for our own programming.

LESSONS LEARNED

Introducing online teaching to both librarians and teaching faculty is an adventure to say the least, and as we have begun to make some moves in that direction, we have learned a couple of things that we thought you might find interesting.

Marketing is Crucial

Not only do you have to make sure you advertise any drop in online workshops you plan to offer, but you also need to let faculty know that you are capable of creating either tutorials or online synchronous workshops. If you are planning a series of perhaps lunchtime online drop-in workshops, you will want to lay out the schedule for these at the beginning of the semester and allow plenty of time for advertising. You will also want to plan these to coincide with any academic milestones during the semester like midterms and exams. This will allow you to attract attention with your marketing by speaking directly to students' needs. For example, a workshop might be pitched by saying: "Need to find two more sources for your paper? Come to our fifteen-minute online workshop to find out where to get reliable citations that will surely impress your professor!" You will also want to make sure that you are diversifying your marketing material by advertising on library blogs and websites but also by putting up fliers both inside and outside the library. If your workshops target a certain population, such as graduate students, go and find the graduate student offices and post fliers on bulletin boards. You might also think about sending an email to graduate student coordinators and asking them to pass the information along to their advisees. If your classes are more general in nature, you may contact other trainers on campus and ask if they would mind letting students know about your training calendar or registration system before, during, or after their own training with assurance that you will do the same for them in your sessions.

Not only will you need to advertise any drop-in workshops, you will also want to be sure that teaching faculty know that you now have the ability to create an online learning experience for their classes. One idea might be to search for any syllabi in your subject areas in syllabus repositories for assignments that might benefit from a quick library session. Based on the assignment, you could contact the faculty member and suggest an outline for a workshop. You might also consider reaching out to any senior seminar type classes or those general education classes, such as introductory English courses where you know that writing and research will be involved.

Whether you are planning for general or targeted online teaching, you must make sure that your constituents know that these opportunities exist. Preparing to teach online takes a great deal of time and effort, so you want to make sure that both students and faculty are involved and aware of these valuable resources.

Focus on Technology Integration, Digital Literacy, and Plagiarism Education

Student projects are focusing increasingly on technology and, as a result, information needs are changing. We have found here at Clemson that creating workshops that deal with image rights and sources as well as concerns about plagiarism and access to technology are topics that can easily be addressed in the online environment. Even a quick workshop or tutorial to serve as a reminder about the kinds of resources available to support digital projects that the library provides would be integral to many classes that incorporate these kinds of assignments. Examples of workshops that might cover these kinds of topics:

- Critically Evaluating and Utilizing Social Media and Other Popular Sources
- Research and Multimedia Support at Your Library
- Using Twitter for Research
- Finding Free Music for Your YouTube or Other Videos

Patron-Led Scheduling

Another idea that we tried is planning our workshops using a demand-based scheduling model that allows student and faculty demand to drive scheduling decisions. You can do this by creating an online form with a list of all of the workshops you could potentially provide and asking patrons to choose the one(s) they are interested in attending. You can then contact the potential attendees with a Doodle poll or a list of potential times with the request they select the ones that would be best or possible for them.[1] This could be done individually, but it would likely be a better use of time if you were to wait until you had a list of interested students to contact with dates and times. We found that this was helpful since students and faculty plan their days around their classes and it made it easier for our workshops to fit in between those firm commitments.

In-Class Tech Support

This was one of the most crucial lessons that we learned here at Clemson, especially since we were trying to encourage librarians who were very unsure of the online environment. Ensuring that someone is available to assist them in the online classroom means your presenter can focus on the lesson and not be concerned with missing something in the chat or trouble-shooting for that one student who cannot hear the presentation. Our instructional designer was able to attend all of our online workshops and was on hand to deal with any technical issues plus provide added value such as typing in the chat the URL of any websites that were mentioned by the instructor. She also made sure that the sessions were recorded and sent to the attendees. We found this to be very helpful and it keeps the instructor from being distracted and throwing the entire workshop off course.

Keep It Simple

In 2008, the Clemson Libraries had an opportunity to participate in a zero-credit required course for all incoming students. This course included the summer reading program, diversity training, and an hour-long face-to-face library workshop as academic pieces in addition to some expected social events. When we began planning this workshop, we tried to cram in as much information about the library as we could to maximize our opportunity with each student, but we quickly found that this was overwhelming for both our instructors and the students. We also found that a workshop that was not attached to an assignment or a class and was provided at the beginning of the fall semester before students actually needed research information was just not very effective. Over the course of the next couple of years, we decreased the number of outcomes from over twenty to three:

> **Outcome 1** (Library Resources): Student will be able to access library resources and services in order to find resources for college-level research.
> **Outcome 2** (Going beyond Google): Student will be able to use library resources in order to verify/supplement the information that they find on the web.
> **Outcome 3** (Critical Analysis of Materials): Student will be able to assess articles based on learned criteria in order to determine which resources will provide information that is more scholarly.

Each time you plan to teach a workshop, try to focus on one or two outcomes to maximize impact for both instructor and student. It also helps to market your workshops by speaking to students' needs and teaching workshops that address those issues. For example, if you know that there is an assignment coming up where students will have to print posters, work with your technology trainers to offer a package of workshops that address how to print a poster (IT), ensure the content is articulate and properly cited (writing center), and find high-quality images and information sources (library). This offers a one-stop-shopping model for students who are looking for help with a particular project.

SAMPLE WORKSHOP OUTLINES

In this section, we wanted to include some "out of the box" outlines so that you can try an online workshop that has already been used to see how it fits. One of the most labor intensive parts of planning for online teaching is creating the outline and coming up with appropriate activities that make good use of the technology at hand. We are not saying that these are the perfect workshops; they are just ready to try out to get a taste for what might or might not work for your library.

The first thing to remember in teaching online workshops is that you will want to be sure that students are comfortable in the online classroom; at the beginning of any online session, you should take a few minutes to do a technical introduction that might include

- Indicating if the class will be recorded

- Introducing yourself with a photo or webcam and identifying any classroom assistants
- Briefly describing the status indicator methods by which students can communicate with the instructor such as by virtually raising their hand, agreeing/disagreeing, or indicating applause or other states (depending on the platform)
- Introducing chat in the classroom space and how it is to be used during the session (some instructors prefer questions be held until the end, while others are open to questions during the session)

You may also want to take the opportunity at the beginning of each class to ask attendees to type in the chat box what they would like to get out of the session. This data can be used later to assess patron needs and plan for future sessions.

Once you get the technical details out of the way, you can focus on the "meat" of your session. Here is an example of a workshop that focuses on accessing library resources online.

In thirty minutes, we will cover

- Finding articles (OneSearch,[2] Research Guides, Interlibrary Loan, Google Scholar)
- Finding books (Catalog, OneSearch, Google Books, WorldCat)
- Locally-sourced digital collections (online yearbooks, institutional repository)
- Getting help (Ask Us webpage, subject librarians, the library on Blackboard)

Here is an example of a shorter session on technology checkout available from the library:

In fifteen minutes, we will cover

- Available technology (cameras, microphones, projectors, portable DVD player, GPS, iPads, iPad minis, and Xbox 360 and PS4 consoles and games)
- Where to find it (Technology Lending webpage)
- Checkout method (at library services desk with university ID) and times
- Where to ask for more information

At the end of each session, you will want to provide a very brief wrap up and even an assessment. This can include the following reminders:

- Be sure to use available tools
- Remember we can borrow pretty much *anything*
- *Ask for help!*

You will notice that these workshops are brief, much shorter than the ordinary hour or hour and fifteen minutes, and they are quite targeted.

Ideally, you could work with a faculty member within a class to develop an online session that would cover something as specific as using one particular database or showing students how to export records to their RefWorks account from Google Scholar. You could also plan to work with other groups on campus to create a bundle of online sessions that speak to a large campus project or collection of classes. Here is a list of the online workshops that we provided at Clemson in a series we called Online with Librarians (OWL):

- Accessing the Library Online
- Advanced Google Searching
- Apps for Research
- Building a Better Search
- Citing Your Sources
- Plagiarism
- Finding eBooks FAST
- Embedding Articles in Your Courses
- RSS Feeds
- Returning to Research
- Writing a Lit Review
- Find 10 Scholarly Articles on *Anything*
- Learn to Research Like a Librarian

Another consideration might be to include both an online piece and a face-to-face session as you "flip" the library classroom. For example, you could ask that students watch one or two asynchronous tutorials that cover topics you would like them to apply in a face-to-face session, such as how to email articles from the database you would like them to use as well and a quick introduction to some of the finer points of searching said database. This way, you can spend time with the students in class actually working on finding resources instead of starting at the very beginning.

SAMPLE IMPLEMENTATION CALENDAR

As with planning an online workshop, sometimes the most difficult thing to do is to wrap your head around the concept as a whole. Making a change as drastic as moving a series of face-to-face workshops online can appear quite daunting, but a little planning can help make it much less intimidating. Again, we wanted to use this book as a way to supply you with ideas for getting started in your own programming. One suggestion is to take things a semester at a time, start by taking one summer to work toward a fall semester start. Table 10.1 shows a timeline that can serve as a guide for approaching such an implementation.

These are just some suggestions, but hopefully it will give you an idea of ways that you might be able to take manageable bits out of an overwhelming process.

COURSE INTEGRATION

One of the most effective ways to get students involved with online library workshops is through teaching faculty. At Clemson, we recently gained the opportunity to include four library questions in the course evaluation for one of our introductory English classes. While our instructional presence there has so far been face-to-face, what we learned from our first foray into this follow-up method could easily be adjusted to collect data on the integration of online and asynchronous library instruction. As it turns out, we had been invited to provide library instruction for some course sections but not others. The benefit of our incomplete course saturation was that we had some semblance of a control group against which we could compare any gains in student confidence or performance. While we were limited to four questions, we could use a mix of multiple choice, Likert scale, and free text question types. Since the course evaluation is administered as a survey in Blackboard, we were not able to include any conditional display logic. This made question design difficult since we knew a significant percentage of the respondents will not have had any library instruction. While our primary data interest was students who had received library instruction, we did not want to squander the opportunity to get feedback from others. This kind of course involvement will allow the libraries to more closely integrate online instruction as well as gather some clear connections to student success.

TEACHING WITH TECHNOLOGY

The main library at Clemson is now home to three major technology support entities: the main IT support desk, the Adobe Digital Studio, and a geographic information system (GIS) lab. There are many ways that librarians can work with these groups to enhance the instructional experience for patrons. One of the most simple would be to meet with the primary trainers in these areas and discuss ways that each group can advertise the training of the other groups at some point in their training session. For example, if the GIS lab holds a session about a software program, they might take a few minutes at the beginning or end of the class to mention other sessions being offered by the library on how to collect data to map in their projects or an Excel class offered by the IT support group that will help them manage the data. Another opportunity could come from bundling workshops, as mentioned previously, for particular projects or assignments. For institutions with off-campus pro-

Table 10.1.

May	• Gather library instruction personnel for a discussion about a potential move to online workshops. Use prepared questions to guide the conversation. • Gather student input about needs/wants for online session topics.
June	• Conduct training sessions in the online classroom, showing instructors tools and pedagogical ideas about teaching in this environment. • Begin planning outlines for online sessions, including templates and accessibility considerations for all content.
July	• Devise marketing plan by deciding what kinds of advertising you will use and when it will be distributed. Include in this plan a timeline for release dates of blog and social media posts and distribution of print fliers. • Place workshops on a calendar, planning to release them during key times in the semester. • Plan for follow-up meetings with online instructors to ensure their comfort level with the move online. • Provide practice sessions for "dry runs" of workshops.
August	• Create internal awareness among employees (and volunteers) so that everyone knows about workshops and can direct patrons to them as the semester progresses. • Begin marketing and build excitement about upcoming workshops.
September–November	• Ensure that workshop assessment data is being collected as planned. • Attend workshops to observe and provide structured feedback to instructors (see figure 9.1 in chapter 9 for sample rubric). • Encourage instructors to attend each other's sessions to observe and gather ideas for their own teaching.

December	• Aggregate assessment data and analyze it for trends and opportunities. • Share individual feedback with instructors and schedule additional training as needed. • Create a report to share with both instructors and with library administration. • Adjust plans for next semester as indicated by data and administrator feedback on report.

grams, the libraries and technology trainers might plan to team up for a "Road Show" and plan presentations for groups who are in other locations to help them understand how they can utilize campus support from a distance.

FITTING INTO THE BIG PICTURE

Last and arguably most important is the effort that needs to be placed in fitting these online workshops into the larger library and university goals. The clear articulation of roles that these workshops will play in achieving institutional goals will increase their visibility and impact. Take time to find your unit, library, and university goals and use your annual or even biannual instruction report to show how your workshops are helping to meet those goals. As links to student success from the library become sought after by library administration, this kind of connection can become very powerful. Here at Clemson Libraries, we are focused on the developing plan for the university as a whole and how we might best fit into that vision. For example, included in the university plan is an extensive conversation about scholarly impact and metrics. This is an area where librarians could play a vital role and the development of online educational pieces about altmetric tools, traditional scholarly metrics, our institutional repository, and rights management considerations would be of great use to an institution moving in this direction.

The bottom line out of everything we have discussed in this book is to try something different. Even if you just begin a conversation with your library instructors and find that online workshops are not an appropriate avenue for your library to explore at this time, you will have at least sparked some ideas for new directions. The road may not be easy and there will likely be setbacks along the way. Here at Clemson, we have struggled with attendance in our online workshops and with faculty integration, but we keep trying different approaches. We keep our ears to the ground and listen to those around us as we gather new ideas to try in our own environment. You must listen to both internal and external audiences in the process, so starting conversations with your library instructors will be just as important as listening to others on campus. It is also our hope that this book will give you some places to start because sometimes starting can be the hardest part, especially when crucial and sometimes difficult conversations are an integral part of that beginning. That is what this book was meant to be: a place to look for ideas. It is not something to follow to the letter, but rather somewhere to look for a glimpse of inspiration and empathy. Library instruction is moving in new directions, and we are all just along for the ride. Enjoy!

NOTES

1. Easy Scheduling, *Doodle*, accessed November 23, 2015, www.doodle.com.
2. The federated search tool used by Clemson University Libraries.

Appendix 1

Sample Focus Group Script and Question Sheet

Note: This document is formatted for a single person to both lead the session and record the data. For ease of use, anticipated simple responses were typed in all caps with a blank space afterward for tallying via hash marks.

Thank you for coming to our student focus group! Please read and complete a consent form.

    I am _____ and I am going to ask you some questions. Please give your honest opinion and provide as much detail as you can. I will be taking notes, but everything you say will be confidential. This will take 30 minutes and then you'll receive your gift card.

Let's get started!

1. How do you currently use the library?

2. What do you like about Clemson Libraries? *[What have we been doing right?]*

3. What can the library do to help make it easier to finish last-minute projects?

4. How do you want to find out what the library can do to help?

5. What kind of advertising on campus gets your attention? *[signs, fliers, table tents]*

6. Would you attend a face-to-face library workshop?
    YES: What topic(s) would interest you?
    NO: Why not?

7. . . . an online library workshop? *[you log in on your computer/ device for a live session]*
    YES: Is there a specific time of day that would be best?
    NO: Why not?

8. Would you watch a library tutorial? *[a less-than-3-minute video you can access anytime]*

    YES: What topic(s) would interest you?
    NO: Why not?

9. Have you ever asked a library person a question?
    NO:
    YES: What was it?

10. Do you search for "how to" videos on YouTube?
    NO:
    YES: What is one of your favorites?

11. When's the last time you visited the library webpage (clemson.edu/library)?
    UNK/NEVER:
        a. Did you find what you needed?
            YES: NO:
        b. Was it easy to use?
            YES: NO:

12. Please briefly describe the process you go through when you get a research assignment or have to write a paper.

13. What library service(s) do you use the most?

14. Did you know that you can text a librarian?
    NO
    YES: Have you ever?
        YES
        NO: Would you?
            YES:
            NO: Why not?

15. Do you use Twitter?
    NO
    YES: Did you know that we're on Twitter?
        NO:
        YES: Do you follow us on Twitter?
            YES:
            NO: Why not?

16. What do you feel would make you more likely to visit the library/use library services?

17. Would you be interested in participating in contests?
    NO: Why not?
    YES: Please briefly describe what type would interest you.

18. When do you come into the library?
    a. Never
    b. What's the best time to come to the library?

c. Where do you go when you come here?

19. What would make you more likely to contact the library for help?

20. What would make library staff more approachable?

21. Do you have any other suggestions, recommendations, or frustrations about Clemson Libraries?

Appendix 2

Excerpt of Aggregated Data from Student Focus Groups

Note: Unless otherwise indicated with a parenthetical number, response was given once.

What can the library do to help make it easier to finish last-minute projects?

- Wi-fi, faster (3)
- Printers, more (2)
- Coffee shop hours, extend
- Plotting, decrease turnaround time
- Computers, faster boot from login
- Group space, more
- Provide good environment for using specific CAD software
- Sources, help me get more

How do you want to find out what the library can do to help?

- Website (4)
- Email (3) — monthly or per semester
- Tweet (2)
- Post in library study areas (2)
- Digital display wall in lobby (2)
- App
- Instagram
- Via Google Scholar

Would you attend an online library workshop?
   [you log in on your computer/device for a live session]

- Yes (9) — prefer to in-person (3), after lunch (2), prefer midday/noon, evening, morning, not before 10 a.m., 2–3 p.m., before 5 p.m., definitely not Friday or Monday
- No (3)

Would you watch a library tutorial?
   [a less-than-3-minute video you can access anytime]

- Yes (14) — APA/MLA formatting (2), how to book a room, RefWorks, ReadCube, things the library has, profiles of specific resources, ILL, finding standards, patent application info
- No — would prefer an FAQ/ help page

Have you ever asked a library person a question?

- Yes (11) — technology checkout (2), how to fax/ scan, if there is a space to store things temporarily, get an audiobook, help finding a book, when is something due, location question, checkout, research
- No (4)

Do you ever search for "how to" videos on YouTube or Google?

- Yes (14) — Khan Academy (2), Howcast for general how-to's
- No — prefer to read about it

When's the last time (if ever) you visited the library webpage? *[clemson.edu/library]*

- Within the past school year (6)
- Within the last week (6)
- Within the past day
- Never

Please briefly describe the process you go through when you get a research assignment or have to write a paper.

- Google/Google Scholar (10)
- Visit library website to access database (3)
- PubMed
- Visit the library

Appendix 3

Sample Extension Agent Survey

Note: Circles indicate single-response question types and squares indicate select multi-select questions.

1. What is your current position?

    o Faculty or staff
    o Student

2. How many times a month do you access resources from a library, either in person or online?

    o 1–2
    o 3–4
    o More than 4
    o None

3. If you do not use the Clemson Libraries often, why?

    □ Didn't know what resources were there
    □ Not sure how to use the library
    □ Tried before but didn't find what I was looking for
    □ Library resources not needed for my work
    □ I find all my information on the web
    □ I use other libraries. If so, which ones?
    □ Other (please specify)

4. When you need to find information, what is the primary tool that you use?

    o Library website
    o Direct electronic journal or database access
    o Google
    o Cooperative Extension webpages
    o Other (please specify):

5. Where are you physically located when you are searching for information:

    □ In the field

Appendix 3

- ☐ In your office
- ☐ At home
- ☐ On campus
- ☐ In the library

6. What library services or materials could be provided that would meet your needs?

- ☐ Access to current journal articles online
- ☐ Access to older journal articles online
- ☐ Access to older images
- ☐ Access to books
- ☐ Access to reliable information on agricultural topics
- ☐ Videos
- ☐ Instruction on finding resources from the library
- ☐ Other (please specify):

7. The libraries offer a variety of ways to teach efficient ways to find quality information. Which type would be most beneficial to you in your work or research?

- o Online library classes
- o Online library tutorials
- o Face-to-face instruction

8. What kinds of workshops would be most useful to you?

- ☐ How to cite
- ☐ How to research in books and articles
- ☐ How to find images
- ☐ How to write abstracts
- ☐ How to conduct literature reviews
- ☐ Advanced Google searching
- ☐ Copyright and plagiarism
- ☐ Accessing online library resources
- ☐ Other (please specify):

9. What time of day would generally be best for you to participate in training?

- o Morning (8 a.m.–12 p.m.)
- o Afternoon (1–4:30 p.m.)
- o Evening (5–9 p.m.)

10. What weekday(s) would be best for you to participate in training?

- ☐ Monday
- ☐ Tuesday
- ☐ Wednesday
- ☐ Thursday

☐ Friday

11. How would you prefer to get news about library resources and services?

  ☐ Email
  ☐ Website
  ☐ Social media (e.g., Facebook, Twitter)
  ☐ Newsletter

12. Please provide any additional comments you may have about library instruction or this survey:

Bibliography

Allen, I. Elaine, and Jeff Seaman. *Changing Course: Ten Years of Tracking Online Education in the United States*. Babson Survey Research Group, 2013.

Bell, Steven, and John Shank. "The Blended Librarian: A Blueprint for Redesigning the Teaching and Learning Role of Academic Librarians." *College & Research Library News* 65, no. 7 (2004): 372–75.

Biddix, J. Patrick, Chung Joo Chung, and Han Woo Park. "Convenience or Credibility? A Study of College Student Online Research Behaviors." *The Internet and Higher Education* 14, no. 3 (2011): 175–82. doi:10.1016/j.iheduc.2011.01.003.

Bury, Sophie. "Faculty Attitudes, Perceptions and Experiences of Information Literacy: A Study across Multiple Disciplines at York University, Canada." *Journal of Information Literacy* 5, no. 1 (2011): 45–64. dx.doi.org/10.11645/5.1.1513.

Catalano, Amy. "Patterns of Graduate Students' Information Seeking Behavior: A Meta-synthesis of the Literature." *Journal of Documentation* 69, no. 2 (2013): 243–74. doi:10.1108/00220411311300066.

Chakraborty, Mou, Michael English, and Sharon Payne. "Restructuring to Promote Collaboration and Exceed User Needs: The Blackwell Library Access Services Experience." *Journal of Access Services* 10, no. 2 (2013): 90–101. doi:10.1080/15367967.2013.762276.

Daland, Hilde. "Just in Case, Just in Time, or Just Don't Bother? Assessment of One-Shot Library Instruction with Follow-Up Workshops." *LIBER Quarterly* 24, no. 3 (2015): 125–39.

Denison, Denise R., and Diane Montgomery. "Annoyance or Delight? College Students' Perspectives on Looking for Information." *The Journal of Academic Librarianship* 38, no. 6 (2012): 380–90. doi:10.1016/j.acalib.2012.08.007.

Ferrero, Guillaume. "L'inertie mentale et la loi du moindre effort." *Revue philosophique de la France et de L'étranger* 37 (1894): 169–82.

Flaherty, Colleen. "So Much to Do, So Little Time," *Inside Higher Ed*. (April 9, 2014), https://www.insidehighered.com/news/2014/04/09/research-shows-professors-work-long-hours-and-spend-much-day-meetings.

Gross, Melissa, and Don Latham. "Experiences with and Perceptions of Information: A Phenomenographic Study of First-Year College Students." *The Library Quarterly: Information, Community, Policy* 81, no. 2 (2011): 161–86. doi:10.1086/658867.

Gross, Melissa, and Don Latham. "What's Skill Got to Do With It? Information Literacy Skills and Self-Views of Ability among First-Year College Students." *Journal of the American Society for Information Science and Technology* 63, no. 3 (2012): 574–83. doi:10.1002/asi.21681.

Gross, Melissa, and Don Latham. "Undergraduate Perceptions of Information Literacy: Defining, Attaining, and Self-Assessing Skills." *College & Research Libraries* 70, no. 4 (2009): 336–50. doi: 10.5860/crl.70.4.336.

Hartman, Teresa L., and Alissa V. Fial. "Creating Interactive Online Instruction: The McGoogan Library Experience." *Medical Reference Services Quarterly* 34, no. 4 (2015): 407–17. doi:10.1080/02763869.2015.1082373.

Henry, Jo. "Academic Library Liaison Programs: Four Case Studies." *Library Review* 61, no. 7 (2012): 485–96. doi:10.1108/00242531211288236.

Hess, Amanda N. "Online and Face-to-Face Library Instruction: Assessing the Impact on Upper-Level Sociology Undergraduates." *Behavioral & Social Sciences Librarian* 33, no. 3 (2014): 132–47. http://hdl.handle.net/10323/3126.

Ince, Sharon, and John Irwin. "LibGuides CMS eReserves: Simplify Delivering Course Reserves through Blackboard." *Interlending & Document Supply* 43, no. 3 (2015): 145–47. doi:10.1108/ILDS-05-2015-0014.

Jaguszewski, Janice, and Karen Williams. "New Roles for New Times: Transforming Liaison Roles in Research Libraries." Report prepared for the Association of Research Libraries, 2013. http://www.arl.org/storage/documents/publications/nrnt-liaison-roles-revised.pdf.

Krishnan, S. Shunmuga and Ramesh K. Sitaraman. "Video Stream Quality Impacts Viewer Behavior: Inferring Causality Using Quasi-Experimental Designs." Paper presented at the 2012 ACM Conference, Boston, MA. doi:10.1145/2398776.2398799.

Kyrillidou, Martha, and Les Bland, eds. *ARL Statistics 2006–2007*. Washington, D.C.: Association of Research Libraries, 2008.

Kyrillidou, Martha, Shaneka Morris, and Gary Roebuck, eds. *ARL Statistics 2012–2013*. Washington, D.C.: Association of Research Libraries, 2014.

Mathews, Brian. "Marketing Today's Academic Library: A Bold New Approach to Communicating with Students." *ALA Editions*, 2009.

Mestre, Lori S. "Student Preference for Tutorial Design: A Usability Study." *Reference Services Review* 40, no. 2 (2012): 258-276. doi:10.1108/00907321211228318.

Purcell, Kristen, Lee Raine, Alan Heaps, Judy Buchanan, Linda Friedrich, Amanda Jacklin, Clara Chen, and Kathryn Zickuhr. "How Teens Do Research in the Digital World." Pew Research Center, 2012. Accessed November 20, 2015. http://www.pewinternet.org/2012/11/01/how-teens-do-research-in-the-digital-world/.

Shank, John D., Steven Bell, and Diane Zabel. "Blended Librarianship: [Re]Envisioning the Role of Librarian as Educator in the Digital Information Age." *Reference & User Services Quarterly* 51, no. 2 (2011): 105–10. http://www.jstor.org/stable/refuseserq.51.2.105.

Taylor, Arthur. "A Study of the Information Search Behaviour of the Millennial Generation." Information Research 17 (1) paper 508, 2012. http://InformationR.net/ir/17-1/paper508.html.

About the Authors

Anne Grant is the instruction coordinator at Clemson University Libraries. She obtained her MLIS from the University of Alabama via their online program in 2007 and has presented at many state and national conferences about innovation and challenges in library instruction.

Diana Finkle is instructional designer for the Clemson University Libraries and earned her MLIS from the University of Alabama, also through its online cohort. A technophile and accessibility advocate, Diana enjoys creating digital content that is appealing, engaging, and user friendly.